ie Worlds

H. G. WELLS

Level 5

Retold by David Maule
Series Editors: Andy Hopkins and Jocelyn Potter

Pearson Education Limited
Edinburgh Gate, Harlow,
Essex CM20 2JE, England
and Associated Companies throughout the world.

ISBN: 978-1-4058-6524-1

First published by Penguin Books 2005
This edition published 2008

1 3 5 7 9 10 8 6 4 2

Original copyright © the Literary Executors of the
Estate of H. G. Wells
Text copyright © Penguin Books Ltd 2005
This edition copyright © Pearson Education Ltd 2008

Typeset by Graphicraft Ltd, Hong Kong
Set in 11/14pt Bembo
Printed in China
SWTC/01

Published by Pearson Education Ltd in association with
Penguin Books Ltd, both companies being subsidiaries of Pearson Plc

For a complete list of the titles available in the Penguin Readers series please write to your local
Pearson Longman office or to: Penguin Readers Marketing Department, Pearson Education,
Edinburgh Gate, Harlow, Essex CM20 2JE, England.

Contents

Introduction

I was not the master now, but an animal among the animals, under the power of the Martians. The rule of man had ended.

At the end of the nineteenth century, a metal object falls from the sky and lands in Woking Common in the south of England. Everyone in town is curious. People come in great numbers to see what it is and surround the hole it has created. When one end of the object starts to open, they realize that it is hollow. Are there men inside? But the creatures that come out are not human.

A group of scientists approaches with a white flag, but they are met with invisible rays. These creatures have weapons that no human being has ever known. Slowly, people begin to understand that these creatures have come from Mars, and that there are more on their way. But why? Do the Martians want to kill everybody on Earth and take the planet for themselves?

News of this strange attack is sent by telegram to London, where it is not taken very seriously at first. By the time the army arrives to control the situation, more spaceships from Mars are arriving with more weapons. Fear turns to panic and people leave their homes in an attempt to get away safely.

Most of the story of *The War of the Worlds* takes place around the town of Woking, to the southwest of London, where H. G. Wells was living when he wrote it. The action then moves north into the centre of London. It is told in the first person by the main character, a writer, who is forced to become a refugee as he tries to escape from the Martians. He reports the events as he experiences them. He also tells us about his brother's experience of trying to escape London, which is told with the information that the storyteller obtains later.

The War of the Worlds appeared in 1898, at the end of a century in which Britain had become the most powerful country in the world. Life, at least for people who had a reasonable amount of money, was comfortable and safe. However, in this story Wells looks forward to the coming century, the twentieth century, and he imagines the possibility of great wars being fought with machines. He imagines roads filling with desperate refugees trying to escape the fighting and he imagines the use of poison gas. When the book first appeared, this was complete science fiction. People did not think that events like the ones in the story could ever happen.

When we read now what Wells wrote more than a hundred years ago, we realize that many of his imaginings were very accurate. How did he know that the world would fight great wars with terrible machines, aeroplanes, and weapons which had the power to destroy whole towns?

Wells understood a great deal about human behaviour and the psychology of terror. He understood the good and the evil that people show in their behaviour. In this story of almost unimaginable events, his characters' actions are always believable. Many ordinary people show great kindness to others when they are in terrible situations. Others only take care of themselves.

H. G. Wells was born on 21 September 1866 in Bromley, south of London. His father, Joseph Wells, and his mother, Sarah, had four children. His father was a professional sportsman, and later a shopkeeper and a gardener. Coming from the lower middle-class, they were not poor but they did not have a lot of opportunities. Wells's mother worked as a servant in a country house near Petersfield.

At the age of seven, Wells had a serious accident and broke his leg. He had to stay in bed for months, so his father made sure that he had a lot of books and magazines to read. Later, Wells said that this period gave him a thirst for knowledge that stayed with him for the rest of his life. A few months after Wells's accident, his father, too, had an accident, which left him unable to play sport. The family then needed the sons to work and earn an income. Wells helped to support the family by working first in the cloth business, then in a chemist's shop and, at the age of sixteen, as a science teacher.

He was then given a free place at a college to study science, and in October 1890 Wells received a first-class degree from the University of London. While he was very interested in many branches of science, he was also interested in society and the social injustices that were common among the working people at that time. These interests led him to read many books on the social affairs and to get involved in political groups.

At the age of twenty-one, Wells had another accident that resulted in another important change in his life. During a football match, one of the students at the school where he taught kicked him very hard in the back. This led to another long period in bed, so he joined his mother at the country house where she worked and took every opportunity to read books from her employer's library. While he recovered, he had the time to write. Wells was very interested in scientific progress, which was leading to new and wonderful discoveries all the time at the end of the nineteenth century, but he could see the possible dangers in these discoveries as well as the advantages and he often wrote about these concerns.

Wells's first novel, *The Time Machine*, appeared in 1895 and was an immediate success. He also wrote short stories, often humorous, for newspapers and magazines. Not everything that he produced was science fiction. Novels like *Kipps* (1905), *Tono-Bungay* (1909) and *The History of Mr Polly* (1910) take their stories from the difficult times he had in early life. But he is best known for his science fiction. *The War of the Worlds, The Time Machine, The Island of Doctor Moreau* (1896), *The Invisible Man* (1897), *The*

Sleeper Awakes (1899) and *The First Men in the Moon* (1901) are still widely read and enjoyed all over the world. *The Time Machine, The Island of Doctor Moreau* and *The Invisible Man* are also Penguin Readers.

In 1891 Wells married his cousin, Isabel Wells, but the marriage did not last long. Two years later, he ran away with Amy Catherine Robbins, who he always called 'Jane'. In 1895, he separated from his wife legally and married Jane. They had two sons, but Wells was not a faithful husband. He was strongly attracted to intelligent, independent women. In 1906 he met Amber Reeves, then a science student at Cambridge, and in 1909 she gave birth to Wells's daughter. In 1912, he met Rebecca West, a writer, and they had a son two years later. Wells's novel *Marriage* (1912) lost him a few friends, including the writer George Bernard Shaw. In 1920 Wells fell in love with his translator, Moura Budberg, when he visited Gorky in Russia. But his marriage to Jane continued. When he learned from his son that she was dying, he stayed at home with her for the last six months of her life. Jane Wells died in 1927. Moura Budberg never married Wells, but she stayed with him until his own death twenty years later.

On 30 October 1938, in the United States, in time for Halloween, the actor Orson Welles made a radio broadcast and read parts of *The War of the Worlds*. In his broadcast, though, the Martians attacked New Jersey, in the northeast of the United States. When listeners turned on their radios after the programme had started and heard about the Martians' arrival, they panicked. Tens of thousands of people thought it was a real attack. In fact, it was even interrupted by an announcer reading a report of the day's other news, so it did seem very real.

The unexpected effect of this broadcast shocked the country and the rest of the world. People all over the eastern United States got into their cars and tried to escape. Some had wet towels over their heads to protect them from the Martians' poison gas. When

H. G. Wells heard about the broadcast, he was not very pleased. But when he went to the United States and met Orson Welles, he got a very good impression of the young actor and liked him immediately.

Although the film rights to *The War of the Worlds* were bought by Cecil B. DeMille in 1925, the story was not filmed until 1953, when it was in full colour and contained some exciting battle scenes. The 2005 film, starring Tom Cruise and directed by Steven Spielberg, is set in present-day New Jersey, in the United States, and has the very latest in special effects.

Wells lived through the two world wars and saw the terrible effects of allowing individuals too much power. One of his last books, *The Holy Terror* (1939), was a study of the careers of Stalin, Mussolini and Hitler. After two years of poor health, he died suddenly and quietly in his bed on 13 August 1946.

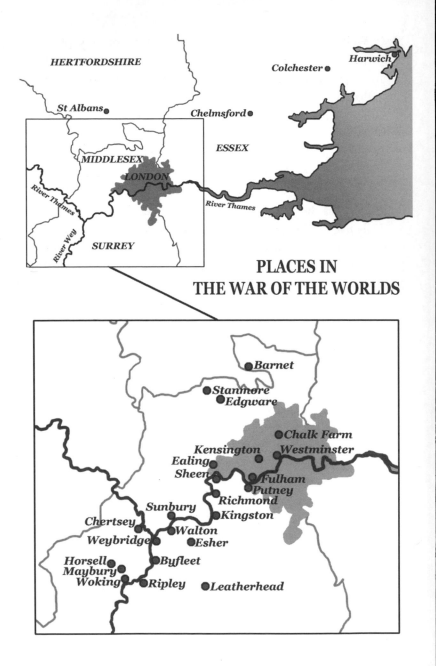

PLACES IN
THE WAR OF THE WORLDS

Chapter 1 Before the War

In the last years of the nineteenth century, no one believed that this world was being watched closely by intelligences greater than our own. We had no idea that we were being studied almost as carefully as a scientist studies the small creatures in a drop of water. With great confidence, people travelled around this world and believed that they were in control of their lives. No one gave a thought to possible threats from other planets.

At most, people believed there might be living things on Mars, perhaps less developed than us and ready to welcome visitors. But across the great emptiness of space, more intelligent minds than ours looked at this Earth with jealous eyes, and slowly and surely made their plans against us. And early in the twentieth century, the great shock came.

The planet Mars, I need not remind the reader, goes around the sun at an average distance of 224,000,000 kilometres, and receives from the sun half of the light and heat that is received by this world. It must be, if scientific thinking is correct, older than our world, and life on its surface began a long time before this Earth cooled down. Because it is hardly one seventh of the size of Earth, it cooled more quickly to the temperature at which life could begin. It has air and water and all that is necessary to support living things.

But people are so blind that no writer, before the end of the nineteenth century, suggested that much more intelligent life had developed there than on Earth. It was also not generally understood that because Mars is older and smaller than our Earth, and further from the sun, it is nearer life's end as well as further from its beginning.

Mars is getting colder, as one day our planet must too. Its

1

physical condition is still largely a mystery, but we know that even in the middle of the day, in its warmest areas, the temperature is lower than during our coldest winter. Its air is much thinner than ours, its oceans have become smaller until they cover only a third of its surface, and from its far north and south the ice is steadily moving forwards. The end of all life, which is a distant possibility for us, is an immediate problem for the Martians.

This has brightened their intelligence, increased their abilities and hardened their hearts. And looking across space, with instruments and minds more powerful than we can dream of, they see, at a distance of only 56,000,000 kilometres, a morning star of hope – our own warmer planet with its green land and grey seas, its cloudy atmosphere and its growing population.

We, the people who live on this Earth, must seem to them at least as different and less developed as monkeys are to us. And before we criticize them for thinking in this way, we must remember how badly we have treated not only the animals of this planet, but also other people. Can we really complain that the Martians treated us in the same way?

It seems that the Martians calculated their journey very cleverly – their mathematical knowledge appears to be much more developed than ours. During 1894, a great light was seen on the surface of the planet by a number of astronomers. I now believe that this was a fire built to make an enormous gun in a very deep pit. From this gun, their shots were fired at us.

The attack came six years ago. Towards midnight on 12 August, one astronomer noticed a great cloud of hot gas on the surface of the planet. In fact, he compared it to the burning gases that might rush out from a gun.

This, we now know, was a very accurate description. However, the next day there was no report in the newspapers except one small note in the *Daily Telegraph*, and the world knew nothing of one of the greatest dangers that ever threatened Earth.

I do not think I would have known anything about it myself if I had not met Ogilvy, the well-known astronomer. He was very excited at the news and invited me to spend the night with him, watching the red planet.

Despite everything that has happened since, I still remember that night very clearly. Looking through the telescope, I saw a circle of deep blue with the little round planet in the centre. Because it was so small, I did not see the Thing they were sending us, which was flying quickly towards me across that great distance. I never dreamed of it then, as I watched. Nobody on Earth knew anything about the approaching missile.

That night, too, there was another sudden cloud of gas from the distant planet as a second missile started on its way to Earth from Mars, just under twenty-four hours after the first one. I saw a reddish flash at the edge, the slightest bend in its shape, as the clock struck midnight.

I remember how I sat there in the blackness, not suspecting the meaning of the tiny light I had seen and all the trouble that it would cause me. I told Ogilvy, and he took my place and watched the cloud of gas growing as it rose from the surface of the planet. He watched until one, and then we lit the lamp and walked over to his house.

Hundreds of observers saw the flame that night and the following night, at about midnight, and again the night after that. For ten nights they saw a flame each night. No one on Earth has attempted to explain why the shots ended after this. It may be that the gases from the firing caused the Martians inconvenience. Thick clouds of smoke or dust, which looked like little grey, moving spots through a powerful telescope on Earth, spread through the clearness of the planet's atmosphere and hid its more familiar features.

Even the daily papers woke up to these events at last, and there was much discussion of their cause. But no one suspected the truth, that the Martians had fired missiles, which were now rushing towards us at a speed of many kilometres a second across the great emptiness of space.

It seems to me almost unbelievably wonderful that, with that danger threatening us, people could continue their ordinary business as they did. One night, when the first missile was probably less than 15,000,000 kilometres away, I went for a walk with my wife. I pointed out Mars, a bright spot of light rising in the sky, towards which so many telescopes were pointing.

The night was warm. Coming home, a group of party-goers from Chertsey passed us, singing and playing music. There were lights in the upper windows of the houses as people went to bed. From the distant railway station came the sound of trains. The world seemed so safe and peaceful.

Chapter 2   The Falling Star

Only a few nights later, the first falling star was seen towards the east. Denning, our greatest astronomer, said that the height of its first appearance was about one hundred and fifty kilometres. It seemed to him that it fell to Earth about a hundred kilometres east of him.

I was at home at the time and writing in my study with the curtains open. If I had looked up I would have seen the strangest thing that ever fell to Earth from space, but I did not. Many people in that part of England saw it, and simply thought that another meteorite had fallen. Nobody went to look for the fallen star that night.

But poor Ogilvy had seen it fall and so he got up very early with the idea of finding it. This he did, soon after dawn. An enormous hole had been made and the Earth had been thrown violently in every direction, forming piles that could be seen two kilometres away.

The Thing itself lay almost completely buried in the earth. The uncovered part looked like an enormous cylinder, about thirty metres across each end. It was covered with a thick burnt skin, which softened its edges. He approached it, surprised at the size and even more surprised at the shape, since most meteorites are fairly round. It was, however, still very hot from its flight through the air and he could not get close to it. He could hear movement from inside but thought this was due to it cooling down. He did not imagine that it might be hollow.

He remained standing on one side of the pit that the Thing had made for itself, staring at its strange appearance and thinking that there might be some intelligent design in its shape. He was alone on the common.

Then suddenly, he noticed that some of the burnt skin was falling off the round edge at the end. A large piece suddenly came off with a sharp noise that brought his heart into his mouth. For a minute he hardly realized what this meant, and although the heat was great, he climbed down into the pit to see the cylinder more closely. He realized that, very slowly, the round top of the cylinder was turning.

Even then he hardly understood what was happening, until he heard another sound and saw the black mark jump forwards a little. Then he suddenly understood. The cylinder was artificial – hollow – with an end that screwed out! Something inside the cylinder was unscrewing the top!

'Good heavens!' said Ogilvy. 'There's a man in it – men in it! Half burnt to death! Trying to escape!'

At once, thinking quickly, he connected the Thing with the flash on Mars.

The thought of the creature trapped inside was so terrible to him that he forgot the heat, and went forwards to the cylinder to help. But luckily the heat stopped him before he could get his hands on the metal. He stood undecided for a moment, then climbed out of the pit and started to run into Woking.

The time then was around six o'clock. He met some local people who were up early, but the story he told and his appearance were so wild that they would not listen to him. That quietened him a little, and when he saw Henderson, the London journalist, in his garden, he shouted over the fence and made himself understood.

'Henderson,' he called, 'you saw that meteorite last night?'

'Yes,' said Henderson. 'What about it?'

'It's out on Horsell Common now.'

'Fallen meteorite!' said Henderson. 'That's good.'

'But it's something more than a meteorite. It's a cylinder – an artificial cylinder! And there's something inside.'

'What did you say?' he asked. He was deaf in one ear.

When Ogilvy told him all he had seen, Henderson dropped his spade, put on his jacket and came out into the road. The two men hurried back at once to the common, and found the cylinder still lying in the same position. But now the sounds inside had stopped, and a thin circle of bright metal showed between its top and body.

They listened, knocked on the burnt metal with a rock and, getting no answer, they both decided that the men inside were either unconscious or dead.

Of course the two were quite unable to do anything, so they went back to the town again to get help. Henderson went to the railway station at once, to send a telegram to London.

By eight o'clock a number of boys and unemployed men were already walking to the common to see the 'dead men from Mars'. That was the form the story took. I heard it first from my newspaper boy at about a quarter to nine and I went to the common immediately.

When I got there, I found a little crowd of perhaps twenty

people surrounding the great pit in which the cylinder lay. Henderson and Ogilvy were not there. I think they understood that nothing could be done for the moment, and had gone away to have breakfast at Henderson's house. I climbed into the pit and thought I heard a faint movement under my feet. The top had certainly stopped turning.

At that time it was quite clear in my own mind that the Thing had come from the planet Mars, and I felt impatient to see it opened. At about eleven, as nothing was happening, I walked back, full of such thoughts, to my home in Maybury.

By the afternoon the appearance of the common had changed very much. The early editions of the evening papers had shocked London. They printed stories like:

MESSAGE RECEIVED FROM MARS
AMAZING STORY FROM WOKING

There was now a large crowd of people standing around. Going to the edge of the pit, I found a group of men in it – Henderson, Ogilvy, and a tall fair-haired man I afterwards learnt was Stent, the Astronomer Royal, with several workmen holding spades. Stent was giving directions. A large part of the cylinder had now been uncovered, although its lower end was still hidden in the side of the pit.

As soon as Ogilvy saw me, he called me to come down, and asked me if I would mind going over to see Lord Hilton, who owned the land. The growing crowd, he said, was now becoming a serious problem, especially the boys. He wanted a fence put up to keep the people back.

I was very glad to do as he asked. I failed to find Lord Hilton at his house, but was told he was expected from London by the six o'clock train. As it was then about a quarter past five, I went home, had some tea and walked up to the station to meet him.

Chapter 3   The Cylinder Opens

When I returned to the common, the sun was setting. Groups of people were hurrying from the direction of Woking. The crowd around the pit had increased to a couple of hundred people, perhaps. There were raised voices, and some sort of struggle appeared to be going on around the pit. As I got nearer, I heard Stent's voice:

'Keep back! Keep back!'

A boy came running towards me.

'It's moving,' he said to me as he passed '– unscrewing and unscrewing. I don't like it. I'm going home.'

I went on to the crowd and pushed my way through. Everyone seemed greatly excited. I heard a peculiar humming sound from the pit.

'Keep those fools back,' said Ogilvy. 'We don't know what's in the Thing, you know.'

I saw a young man – I believe he was a shop assistant in Woking – standing on the cylinder and trying to climb out of the pit again. The crowd had pushed him in.

The end of the cylinder was being screwed out from within. Nearly half a metre of shining screw stuck out. Someone pushed against me, and I almost fell down on top of the screw. I turned, and as I did the screw came out and the lid of the cylinder fell onto the sand with a ringing sound. I pressed back against the person behind me, and turned my head towards the Thing again. I had the sunset in my eyes and for a moment the round hole seemed black.

I think everyone expected to see a man come out – possibly something a little unlike us on Earth, but more or less a man. I know I did. But, looking, I soon saw something grey moving within the shadow, then two shining circles – like eyes. Then something like a little grey snake, about the thickness of a walking-stick, came out of the middle and moved through the air towards me – and then another.

I suddenly felt very cold. There was a loud scream from a woman behind. I half-turned, still keeping my eyes on the cylinder, from which other tentacles were now coming out, and began pushing my way back from the side of the pit. I saw shock changing to horror on the faces of the people around me, and there was a general movement backwards. I found myself alone, and saw the people on the other side of the pit running off. I looked again at the cylinder, and felt great terror.

A big, greyish round creature, the size, perhaps, of a bear, was rising slowly and painfully out of the cylinder. As it moved up and caught the light, it shone like wet leather. Two large dark-coloured eyes were looking at me steadily. The head of the thing was rounded and had, one could say, a face. There was a mouth under the eyes, and its lipless edge shone wetly. The whole creature was breathing heavily. One tentacle held onto the cylinder; another moved in the air.

Suddenly, the creature disappeared. It had fallen over the edge of the cylinder and into the pit. I heard it give a peculiar cry, and then another of these creatures appeared in the deep shadow of the door.

I turned and ran madly towards the first group of trees, perhaps a hundred metres away. I fell a number of times because I was running with my head turned round. I could not take my eyes away from these creatures.

The common was now covered with small groups of people. They were all very frightened, but still interested in the strange happenings in the pit. Then I saw a round object moving up and down. It was the head of the shop assistant who had fallen in, looking black against the hot western sky. He got his shoulder and knee up, but again he seemed to slip back until only his head was visible. Then he disappeared, and I thought I heard a faint scream. For a moment I wanted to go back and help him, but I was too afraid.

The sun went down before anything else happened. The crowd around the pit seemed to grow as new people arrived. This gave people confidence and as darkness fell, a slow, uncertain movement on the common began. Black figures in twos and threes moved forwards, stopped, watched, and moved again, getting closer and closer to the pit.

And then, coming from the direction of Horsell, I noticed a little black group of men, the first of whom was waving a white flag. They were too far away for me to recognize anyone there, but I learned afterwards that Ogilvy, Stent and Henderson were with others in this attempt at communication. As the group moved forwards, a number of other people started to follow them.

Suddenly, there was a flash of light and bright greenish smoke came out of the pit in three separate clouds, which moved up, one after the other, into the still air.

The smoke (or flame, perhaps, would be a better word for it) was so bright that the deep blue sky overhead seemed to darken as these clouds rose. At the same time we could hear a faint sound, which changed into a long, loud humming noise. Slowly a dark shape rose out of the pit and a beam of light seemed to flash out from it.

Then flashes of bright fire came from the men, and I realized that the Martians were using some kind of invisible ray. Then, by the light of their own burning, I saw each of the men falling, and their followers turning to run.

I stood staring, watching as man after man fell over. As the unseen ray of light passed over them, trees caught fire and even the bushes exploded into flame. And far away to the west I saw flashes of trees and bushes and wooden buildings suddenly set on fire.

This flaming death, this invisible sword of heat, was sweeping round quickly and steadily. I knew it was coming towards me because of the flashing bushes it touched, but I was too shocked to move. All along a curving line beyond the pit, the dark ground smoked. Then the humming stopped and the black, rounded object sank slowly out of sight into the pit.

All this happened so quickly that I stood without moving, shocked by the flashes of light. If that death had swung round a full circle, it would have killed me. But it passed and let me live, and left the night around me suddenly dark and unfamiliar. There was nobody else around. Overhead the stars were coming out, and in the west the sky was still a pale, bright, almost greenish blue. The tops of the trees and the roofs of Horsell were sharp and black against the western sky. Areas of bush and a few trees still smoked, and the houses towards Woking station were sending up tongues of flame into the stillness of the evening air.

I realized that I was helpless and alone on this dark common. Suddenly, like a thing falling on me from above, came fear. With an effort I turned and began an unsteady run through the grass.

The fear I felt was panic – terror not only of the Martians but of the dark and stillness all around me. I ran crying silently as a child might do. After I had turned, I did not dare look back.

Chapter 4   Mars Attacks

I ran until I was totally exhausted and I fell down beside the road. That was near the bridge by the gas-works.

I remained there for some time.

Eventually I sat up, strangely puzzled. For a moment, perhaps, I could not clearly understand how I came there. My terror had fallen from me like a piece of clothing. A few minutes earlier there had only been three things in my mind: the great size of the night and space and nature, my own weakness and unhappiness, and the near approach of death. Now I was my normal self again

11

– an ordinary citizen. The silent common, my escape, the flames, seemed like a dream. I asked myself if these things had really happened. I could not believe it.

I got up and walked up the steep slope to the bridge. My body seemed to have lost its strength. The figure of a workman carrying a basket appeared. Beside him ran a little boy. He passed me, wishing me good-night. I thought about speaking to him, but did not. I answered his greeting and went on over the bridge.

Two men and a woman were talking at the gate of one of the houses. I stopped.

'What news from the common?' I said.

'Eh?' said one of the men, turning.

'What news from the common?' I repeated.

'Haven't you just been there?' the men asked.

'People seem fairly silly about the common,' the woman said over the gate. 'What's it all about?'

'Haven't you heard of the men from Mars?' I said. 'The creatures from Mars.'

'Quite enough,' said the woman. 'Thanks.' And all three of them laughed.

I felt foolish and angry. I tried but could not tell them what I had seen. They laughed again at my broken sentences.

'You'll hear more soon,' I said, and went on to my home.

My wife was shocked when she saw me, because I looked so tired and dirty. I went into the dining-room, sat down, and told her the things that I had seen.

'There is one good thing,' I said, to calm her fears. 'They are the slowest, fattest things I ever saw crawl. They may stay in the pit and kill people who come near them, as they cannot get out of it . . . but they are so horrible!'

'Don't, dear!' said my wife, putting her hand on mine.

'Poor Ogilvy!' I said. 'He may be lying dead there.'

My wife, at least, did not think my experience unbelievable.

When I saw how white her face was, I began to comfort her and myself by repeating all that Ogilvy had told me about the impossibility of Martians capturing the Earth.

On the surface of the Earth the force of gravity is three times as great as on the surface of Mars. A Martian, therefore, would weigh three times more than on Mars, although his strength would be the same. That was the general opinion. Both *The Times* and the *Daily Telegraph*, for example, said this very confidently the next morning. Both ignored, as I did, two obvious problems with this theory.

The atmosphere of Earth, we now know, contains much more oxygen than there is on Mars. This certainly gave the Martians much greater strength. And we also learned that the Martians were so mechanically clever that they did not need to use their bodies very much.

But I did not consider these points at the time, and so I thought the Martians had very little chance of success. With wine and food and the need to help my wife feel less afraid, I slowly became braver and felt safer.

I remember the dinner table that evening very clearly even now: my dear wife's sweet, worried face looking at me from under the pink lamp-shade, the white cloth laid with silver and glass, the glass of red wine in my hand. I did not know it, but that was the last proper dinner I would eat for many strange and terrible days.

If, on that Friday night, you had drawn a circle at a distance of five kilometres from Horsell Common, I doubt if there would have been one human being outside it, unless it was a relation of Stent, whose emotions or habits were affected by the new arrivals. Many people had heard of the cylinder, of course, and talked about it, but it did not have as much effect as a political event.

Even within the five-kilometre circle, most people were unaffected. I have already described the behaviour of the people to whom I spoke. All over the district people were eating dinner. Men were gardening, children were being put to bed, young people were out walking together.

Maybe there was talk in the village streets, a new topic in the pubs – and here and there a messenger, or even an eye-witness of the later events, caused some excitement. However, for most of the time the daily routine of work, food, drink and sleep went on as it had done for countless years.

People came to the common and left it, but all the time a crowd remained. One or two adventurous people went into the darkness and crawled quite near the Martians, but they never returned, because now and again a light-ray swept round the common, and the Heat-Ray was ready to follow. And all night the sound of hammering could be heard as the Martians worked on the machines they were making ready.

At about eleven, a company of soldiers came through Horsell and spread out in a great circle around the common. Several officers had been on the common earlier in the day and one was reported to be missing. Another one arrived and was busy questioning the crowd at midnight. The army was certainly taking things seriously.

A few seconds after midnight the crowd in the Chertsey Road, Woking, saw a star fall from the sky into the woods to the north-west. This was the second cylinder.

Saturday lives in my memory as a day of worry. It was a lazy, hot day too. I had only slept a little and I got up early. I went into my garden and stood listening, but towards the common there was nothing moving.

The milkman came as usual and I asked him the latest news. He told me that during the night the Martians had been surrounded by soldiers and that field-guns were expected.

'We have to try not to kill them,' he said, 'if it can possibly be avoided.'

After breakfast, instead of working, I decided to walk down towards the common. Under the railway bridge I found a group of soldiers – engineers, I think, men wearing small round caps, dirty red jackets and dark trousers. They told me that no one was allowed over the bridge. I talked with them for a time and told them of my sight of the Martians on the previous evening. None had seen them, so they asked me many questions. An ordinary engineer is much better educated than a common soldier, and they discussed, with some intelligence, the odd conditions of the possible fight.

After some time I left them and went on to the railway station to get as many morning papers as I could. These contained only very inaccurate descriptions of the killing of Stent, Henderson, Ogilvy and the others. I got back to lunch at about two, very tired because, as I have said, the day was extremely hot and dull. To make myself feel better I took a cold bath in the afternoon.

During that day the Martians did not show themselves. They were busy in the pit, and there was the sound of hammering and a column of smoke. 'New attempts have been made to signal, but without success,' was how the evening papers later described it. An engineer told me that this was done by a man crawling forwards with a flag on a long pole. The Martians took as much notice of him as we would of a cow.

At about three o'clock I heard the sound of a gun, firing regularly, from the direction of Chertsey. I learned that they were shooting into the wood in which the second cylinder had fallen. An hour or two later a field-gun arrived for use against the first cylinder.

At about six in the evening, as I had tea with my wife in the garden, I heard an explosion from the common, and immediately after that the sound of gunfire. Then came a violent crash quite close to us, that shook the ground. I rushed out onto the grass and saw the tops of the trees around the Oriental College burst into smoky red flame, and the tower of the little church beside it slide down into ruins. The roof of the college was in pieces. Then one of our chimneys cracked and broken bricks fell down onto the flower-bed by my study window.

My wife and I stood amazed. Then I realized that the Martians could hit the top of Maybury Hill with their Heat-Ray because they had cleared the college out of the way.

After that I took my wife's arm and ran with her out into the road. Then I went back and fetched the servant.

'We can't stay here,' I said, and as I spoke the firing started again for a moment on the common.

'But where can we go?' said my wife in terror.

I thought, puzzled. Then I remembered my cousins in Leatherhead.

'Leatherhead!' I shouted above the sudden noise.

She looked away from me downhill. Surprised people were coming out of their houses.

'How will we get to Leatherhead?' she asked.

Down the hill I saw some soldiers rush under the railway bridge. Three went through the open doors of the Oriental College and two began running from house to house. The sun, shining through the smoke that rose up from the tops of the trees, seemed blood-red and threw an unfamiliar bright light on everything.

'Wait here,' I said. 'You are safe here.'

I ran at once towards the pub, whose owner had a horse and cart. I ran because I realized that soon everyone on this side of the hill would be moving. I found the pub's owner in his bar, with no idea of what was going on. I explained quickly that I had to leave my home, and arranged to borrow the cart, promising to bring it back before midnight. At the time it did not seem to me so urgent that *he* should leave his home.

I drove the cart down the road and, leaving it with my wife

16

and servant, rushed into the house and packed a few valuables. While I was doing this, a soldier ran past. He was going from house to house, warning people to leave.

I shouted after him, 'What news?'

He turned, stared, shouted something about 'crawling out in a thing like a dish cover', and moved on to the gate of the next house. I helped my servant into the back of the cart, then jumped up into the driver's seat beside my wife. In another moment we were clear of the smoke and the noise, and moving quickly down the opposite side of Maybury Hill.

Chapter 5   Running Away

Leatherhead is about twenty kilometres from Maybury. We got there without any problems at about nine o'clock, and the horse had an hour's rest while I had supper with my cousins and left my wife in their care.

My wife was strangely silent during the drive, and seemed very worried. If I had not made a promise to the pub owner, she would, I think, have asked me to stay in Leatherhead that night. Her face, I remember, was very white as I drove away.

My feelings were quite different. I had been very excited all day and I was not sorry that I had to return to Maybury. I was even afraid that the last shots I had heard might mean the end of our visitors from Mars. I wanted to be there at the death.

The night was unexpectedly dark, and it was as hot and airless as the day. Overhead the clouds were passing fast, mixed here and there with clouds of black and red smoke, although no wind moved the bushes around me. I heard a church strike midnight, and then I saw Maybury Hill, with its tree-tops and roofs black and sharp against the red sky.

At that moment a bright green light lit up the road around me and showed the distant woods to the north. I saw a line of green fire pass through the moving clouds and into the field to my left. It was the third cylinder!

Just after this came the first lightning of the storm, and the thunder burst like a gun overhead. The horse ran forwards in terror at high speed.

There is a gentle slope towards the foot of Maybury Hill, and down this we went. After the lightning had begun, it flashed again and again, as quickly as I have ever seen. The thunder crashed almost all the time. The flashing light was blinding and confusing, and thin rain hit my face as I drove down the slope.

I paid little attention to the road in front of me, and then suddenly my attention was caught by something. At first I thought it was the wet roof of a house, but the lightning flashes showed that it was moving quickly down Maybury Hill. Then there was a great flash like daylight and this strange object could be seen clearly.

How can I describe this Thing that I saw? It was an enormous tripod, higher than many houses, stepping over the young trees. It was a walking engine of shining metal.

Then suddenly, the trees in the wood ahead of me were pushed to the side and a second enormous tripod appeared, rushing, as it seemed, straight towards me. And I was driving fast to meet it. At the sight of this second machine I panicked completely. I pulled my horse's head hard round to the right. The cart turned over on the horse and I was thrown sideways. I fell heavily into a shallow pool of water.

I crawled out almost immediately and lay, my feet still in the water, under a bush. The horse did not move (his neck was broken, poor animal!) and by the lightning flashes I saw the turned-over cart and one wheel still spinning slowly. Then the enormous machine walked past me and went uphill.

As it passed it gave a deafening howl that was louder than the thunder – '*Aloo! Aloo!*' – and a minute later it was with another one, half a kilometre away, bending over something in a field. I have no doubt that this was the third of the cylinders they had fired at us from Mars.

I was wet with rain above and pool-water below. It was some time before my shock would let me struggle up into a drier position, or think of the great danger I was in.

I got to my feet at last and, keeping low, managed to get into a wood near Maybury without the machines seeing me. Staying in the wood, I moved towards my own house. If I had really understood the meaning of all the things I had seen, I would have gone back to join my wife in Leatherhead immediately. But that night it was all very strange and I was physically exhausted, wet to the skin, deafened and blinded by the storm. All these things prevented me from making a sensible decision.

I walked up the narrow road towards my house. Near the top I stood on something soft and, by a flash of lightning, saw the body of a man. I had never touched a dead body before, but I forced myself to turn him over and feel for his heart. He certainly was dead. It seemed that his neck had been broken. Then the lightning flashed again and I saw his face. It was the owner of the pub, whose cart I had taken.

I stepped over him nervously and moved on up the hill. Towards Maybury Bridge there were voices and the sound of feet, but I did not have the courage to shout or go to them. I let myself into my house and locked the door, walked to the bottom of the stairs and sat down, shaking violently.

It was some time before I could get to my feet again and put on some dry clothes. After that I went upstairs to my study. The window looks over the trees and the railway towards Horsell Common. In the hurry to leave it had been left open. I stopped in the doorway, at a safe distance from it.

The thunderstorm had passed. The towers of the Oriental

College and the trees around it had gone. Very far away, lit by red fire, the common was visible. Across the light, great black shapes moved busily backwards and forwards.

I closed the door noiselessly and moved nearer the window. The view opened out until, on one side, it reached to the houses around Woking Station, and on the other, to the burnt woods of Byfleet. Between them were areas of fire and smoking ground. The view reminded me, more than anything else, of factories at night.

I turned my desk chair to the window and stared out at the country and, in particular, at the three enormous black Things that were moving around the common. They seemed very busy. I began to ask myself what they could be. Were they intelligent machines? I felt this was impossible. Or did a Martian sit inside each, controlling it in the same way that a man's brain controls his body?

The storm had left the sky clear, and over the smoke of the burning land the tiny bright light of Mars was dropping into the west, when a soldier came quietly into my garden. I got up and leant out of the window.

'*Pssst!*' I said, in a whisper.

He stopped for a moment, then walked across to the house.

'Who's there?' he said, also whispering.

'Are you trying to hide?' I asked.

'I am.'

'Come into the house,' I said.

I went down, opened the door and let him in. I could not see his face. He had no hat and his coat was unbuttoned.

'What's happened?' I asked.

'We didn't have a chance,' he said. 'Not a chance.'

He followed me into the dining-room.

'Have a drink,' I said, pouring one for him.

He drank it. Then suddenly he sat down at the table, put his head on his arms and began to cry like a little boy. It was a long time before he was able to answer my questions, and the answers he gave were puzzled and came in broken sentences.

He was part of a field-gun team. They were turning their gun to fire on one of the tripods when it suddenly exploded. He found himself lying under a group of burnt dead men and horses. His back was hurt by the fall of a horse and he lay there for a long time. He watched as the foot-soldiers rushed towards the tripod. They all went down in a second. Then the tripod walked slowly over the common. A kind of arm held a complicated metal case, out of which the Heat-Ray flashed as it killed anyone who was still moving. Then the tripod turned and walked away towards where the second cylinder lay.

At last the soldier was able to move, crawling at first, and he got to Woking. There were a few people still alive there; most of them were very frightened, and many of them had been burnt. He hid behind a broken wall as one of the Martian tripods returned. He saw this one go after a man, catch him in one of its steel arms and knock his head against a tree. After it got dark, the soldier finally ran and managed to get across the railway.

That was the story I got from him, bit by bit. He grew calmer telling me. He had eaten no food since midday, and I found some meat and bread and brought it into the room. As we talked, the sky gradually became lighter. I began to see his face, blackened and exhausted, as no doubt mine was too.

When we had finished eating, we went quietly upstairs to my study and I looked again out of the open window. In one night the valley had become a place of death. The fires had died down now, but the ruins of broken and burnt-out houses and blackened trees were clear in the cold light of the dawn. Destruction had never been so total in the history of war. And, shining in the morning light, three of the tripods stood on the common, their tops turning as they examined the damage they had done.

Chapter 6   The Death of Towns

As the dawn grew brighter, we moved back from the window where we had watched and went very quietly downstairs.

The soldier agreed with me that the house was not a good place to stay in. He suggested going towards London, where he could rejoin his company. My plan was to return at once to Leatherhead. The strength of the Martians worried me so much that I had decided to take my wife to the south coast, and leave the country with her immediately. I had already decided that the area around London would be the scene of a great battle before the Martians could be destroyed.

Between us and Leatherhead, however, lay the third cylinder. If I had been alone, I think I would have taken my chance and gone straight across country. But the soldier persuaded me not to. 'It's no kindness to your wife,' he said, 'for you to get killed.' In the end I agreed to go north with him under cover of the woods. After that I would leave him and turn off to reach Leatherhead.

I wanted to start at once, but the soldier had been in wars before and knew better than that. He made me find all the food and drink that we could carry, and we filled our pockets. Then we left the house and ran as quickly as we could down the narrow road. All the houses seemed empty. In the road lay a pile of three burnt bodies close together, killed by the Heat-Ray. In fact, apart from ourselves, there did not seem to be a living person on Maybury Hill.

We reached the woods at the foot of the hill and moved through these towards the road. As we ran, we heard the sound of horses and saw through the trees three soldiers riding towards Woking. We shouted and they stopped while we hurried towards them. They were an officer and two men.

'You are the first people I've seen coming this way this morning,' the officer said. 'What's happening?'

The soldier who had stayed with me stepped up to him. 'My gun was destroyed last night, sir. I've been hiding. I'm trying to rejoin my company. You'll come in sight of the Martians, I expect, about a kilometre along this road.'

'What do they look like?' asked the officer.

'Big machines, sir. Thirty metres high. Three legs and a great big head, sir.'

'What nonsense!' said the officer.

'You'll see, sir. They carry a kind of box that shoots fire and strikes you dead.'

'What do you mean – a gun?'

'No, sir.' And he began to describe the Heat-Ray.

Half-way through his report the officer interrupted him and looked at me.

'Did you see it?' he said.

'It's perfectly true,' I replied.

'Well,' he said, 'I suppose it's my business to see it too. Listen,' he said to my new friend, 'you'd better go to Weybridge and report to the highest officer.'

He thanked me and they rode away.

By Byfleet station we came out from the trees and found the country calm and peaceful in the morning sunlight. It seemed like any other Sunday – except for the empty houses, and the other ones where people were packing.

However, Byfleet was very busy. Soldiers were telling people to leave and helping them to load carts in the main street. Many people, though, did not realize how serious the situation was. I saw one old man with a big box and a number of flower-pots, angrily arguing with a soldier who wanted him to leave them behind.

'Do you know what's over there?' I said, pointing towards the woods that hid the Martians.

'Eh?' he said. 'I was explaining that these are valuable.'

'Death!' I shouted. 'Death is coming! Death!' and leaving him to think about that, I hurried on to Weybridge.

We remained there until midday, and at that time found ourselves at the place where the River Wey joins the River Thames. Here we found an excited crowd of people. There was no great fear at this time, but already there were more people than all the boats could carry across the Thames. Every now and then people looked nervously at the fields beyond Chertsey, but everything there was still.

Then came the sound of a gun and, almost immediately, other guns across the river, unseen because of the trees, began to fire. Everyone stood still, stopped by the sudden sound of battle, near us but invisible to us.

Then we saw a cloud of smoke far away up the river. The ground moved and a heavy explosion shook the air, smashing two or three windows in the houses and leaving us shocked.

'Look!' shouted a man. 'Over there! Do you see them?'

Quickly, one after the other, one, two, three, four of the Martian machines appeared, far away over the low trees towards Chertsey. Then, from a different direction, a fifth one came towards us. Their metal bodies shone in the sun as they moved forwards to the guns. One on the left, the furthest away, held a large case high in the air, and the terrible Heat-Ray shone towards Chertsey and struck the town.

At the sight of these strange, quick and terrible creatures, the crowd near the water's edge seemed for a moment to be totally shocked. There was no screaming or shouting, but a silence. Then came some quiet talk and the beginning of movement. A woman pushed at me with her hand and rushed past me. I turned, but I was not too frightened for thought.

'Get under water!' I shouted, but nobody listened.

I turned around again and ran towards the approaching Martian, ran right down the stony beach and dived into the water. Others did the same. The stones under my feet were muddy and slippery, and the river was so low that I moved perhaps seven metres before I could get under the surface. I could hear people jumping off boats into the water.

But the Martian took no notice of us. When I lifted my head it was looking towards the guns that were still firing across the river. It was already raising the case which sent the Heat-Ray when the first shell burst six metres above its head.

I gave a cry of surprise. Then two other shells burst at the same time in the air near its body. Its head twisted round in time to receive, but not in time to avoid, the fourth shell.

This exploded right in its face. Its head flashed and burst into a dozen broken pieces of red flesh and shining metal.

'Hit!' I shouted.

The headless machine marched on, swinging from side to side. It hit a church tower, knocking it down, then moved on and fell into the river out of sight.

A violent explosion shook the air, and a column of water, steam, mud and broken metal shot far up into the sky. In another moment a great wave of very hot water came sweeping round the bend. I saw people struggling towards the shore and heard their screaming and shouting faintly above the noise of the Martian's fall.

I rushed through the water until I could see round the bend. The Martian came into sight down the river, most of it under the water. Thick clouds of steam were pouring from the wreckage, and through it I could see its long legs and tentacles moving in the water.

My attention was caught by an angry noise. A man, knee-deep in the water, shouted to me and pointed, although I could not hear what he said. Looking back, I saw the other Martians walking down the river-bank from the direction of Chertsey. The guns fired again, but with no effect.

At that moment I got under the water and, holding my breath until movement was painful, swam under the surface for as long as I could. The river was rough around me and quickly growing hotter.

When for a moment I raised my head to breathe and throw the hair and water out of my eyes, the steam was rising in a white fog that hid the Martians completely. The noise was deafening. Then I saw them, enormous grey figures. They had passed me and two were bending over the fallen one.

The third and fourth stood beside him in the water. The cases that produced the Heat-Rays were waved high and the beams flashed this way and that.

The air was full of deafening and confusing noises: the loud sounds of the Martians, the crash of falling houses, the flash of fire as trees and fences began to burn. Thick black smoke was rising to mix with the steam from the river.

Then suddenly the white flashes of the Heat-Ray came towards me. The houses fell as it touched them, and exploded into flame. The trees caught fire with a loud noise. The Heat-Ray came down to the water's edge less than fifty metres from where I stood. It ran across the river and the water behind it boiled. I turned towards the shore.

In another moment a large wave of almost boiling water rushed towards me. I screamed and ran. If my foot had slipped, it would have been the end. I fell in full view of the Martians on the stony beach. I expected only death.

I have a faint memory of the foot of a Martian coming down within twenty metres of my head, going straight into the loose stones. Then I saw the four of them carrying the remains of the fallen one between them, now clear and then later faint through a curtain of smoke, moving away from me across a great space of river and fields. And then, very slowly, I realized that somehow I had escaped.

I saw an empty boat, very small and far away, moving down the river and, taking off most of my wet clothes, I swam to it. I used my hands to keep it moving, down the river towards Walton, going very slowly and often looking behind me. I was in some pain and very tired. When the bridge at Walton was coming into sight, I landed on the Middlesex bank and lay down, very sick, in the long grass.

I do not remember the arrival of the curate, so probably I slept for some time. As I woke up, I noticed a seated figure with his face staring at the sky, watching the sunset.

I sat up, and at the sound of my movement he looked at me.

'Have you any water?' I asked.

He shook his head.

'You have been asking for water for the last hour,' he said.

For a moment we were silent, staring at each other. He spoke suddenly, looking away from me.

'What does it mean? he said. 'What do these things mean?'

I gave no answer.

'Why are these things allowed? What have we done – what has Weybridge done? The morning service was over. I was walking the roads to clear my brain, and then – fire and death! All our work – everything destroyed. The church! We rebuilt it only three years ago. Gone! Why?'

Another pause, and then he shouted, 'The smoke of her burning goes up for ever and ever!' His eyes were wide and he pointed a thin finger in the direction of Weybridge.

It was clear to me that the great tragedy in which he was involved – it seemed that he had escaped from Weybridge – had driven him to the edge of madness.

'Are we far from Sunbury?' I said, very quietly.

'What can we do?' he asked. 'Are these creatures everywhere? Has the Earth been given to them?'

'Are we far from Sunbury?'

'Only this morning I was in charge of the church service –'

'Things have changed!' I said, quietly. 'You must stay calm. There is still hope.'

'Hope!'

'Yes, a lot of hope, despite all this destruction. Listen!'

From beyond the low hills across the water came the dull sound of the distant guns and a far-away strange crying. Then everything was still. High in the west the moon hung pale above the smoke and the hot, still beauty of the sunset.

'We had better follow this path,' I said. 'To the north.'

Chapter 7   In London

My younger brother was in London when the Martians fell at Woking. He was a medical student, working for an examination, and he heard nothing of the arrival until Saturday morning. The morning papers on Saturday contained, in addition to a great deal of information about the planet Mars, one very short report.

The Martians, alarmed by the approach of a crowd, had killed a number of people with a quick-firing gun, the story said. It ended with the words, 'Although they seem frightening, the Martians have not moved from the pit into which they have fallen, and don't seem able to do so.'

Even the afternoon papers had nothing to tell apart from the movement of soldiers around the common, and the burning of the woods between Woking and Weybridge. Nothing more of the fighting was known that night, the night of my drive to Leatherhead and back.

My brother was not worried about us, as he knew from the description in the papers that the cylinder was three kilometres from my house. That night he made up his mind to visit me, in order to see the Things before they were killed. He sent a telegram, which never reached me.

On the Saturday evening, at Waterloo station, he learned that an accident prevented trains from reaching Woking. He could not discover what kind of accident it was. In fact, the people in charge of the railway did not clearly know at that time. There was very little excitement at the station. Few people connected the problem with the Martians.

I have read, in another description of these events, that on Sunday morning 'all London was panicked by the news from Woking.' In fact, this is simply not true. Plenty of Londoners did not hear of the Martians until Monday morning. Some did, but they needed time to realize what all the reports in the Sunday papers actually meant. But most people in London do not read Sunday papers.

Besides this, Londoners are very used to feeling safe, and exciting news is so normal in the papers that they could read reports like this without great fear:

At about seven o'clock last night the Martians came out of the cylinder and, moving around in metal machines, completely destroyed Woking station and the houses around it, and killed around 600 soldiers. No details are known. Machine guns are completely useless against them, and field-guns have been put out of action. The Martians appear to be moving towards Chertsey. People in West Surrey are very worried and defences have been built to slow the Martians' movement towards London.

No one in London knew what the Martians looked like, and there was still a fixed idea that they must be slow: 'crawling', 'moving painfully' – words like these were in all the earlier reports. But none of them were written by anyone who had actually seen a Martian. The Sunday papers printed separate editions as further news came in. But there was almost nothing to tell people until the government announced that the people of Walton and Weybridge, and all that district, were pouring along the roads towards London.

My brother went again to Waterloo station to find out if the line to Woking was open. There he heard that the Chertsey line was also closed. He learned that several unusual telegrams had been received in the morning from Byfleet and Chertsey stations, but that these had suddenly stopped. My brother could get very little exact information out of them. 'There's fighting going on around Weybridge,' was all the information they had.

Quite a number of people who had been expecting friends to arrive by train were standing at the station. One man spoke to my brother.

'There are lots of people coming into Kingston in carts and things, with boxes and cases,' he said. 'They come from Weybridge and Walton, and they said guns have been heard at Chertsey, heavy firing, and that soldiers told them to move out at once because the Martians are coming. What does it all mean? The Martians can't get out of their pit, can they?'

My brother could not tell him.

At about five o'clock the growing crowd in the station was greatly excited by the opening of the line between the South-Eastern and South-Western stations, which is usually closed. Then trains carrying large guns and many soldiers passed through the station, moving towards Kingston. Soon after that the police arrived and began to move the crowd out of the station, and my brother went out into the street again.

On Waterloo Bridge a number of people were watching an odd brown liquid that came down the river from time to time. The sun was just setting and the Houses of Parliament stood against a peaceful sky. There was talk of a floating body.

In Wellington Street my brother met two men selling

newspapers which had just been printed. The advertising boards said, 'Terrible tragedy! Fighting at Weybridge! Defeat of the Martians! London in danger!' He bought a paper.

Then, and only then, he understood something of the full power and terror of the Martians. He learned that they were not just a few small crawling creatures, but that they could control enormous mechanical bodies. They could move quickly and strike with such power that even the biggest guns could not stand against them. They were described as, 'great machines like spiders, nearly thirty metres high, as fast as an express train, and able to shoot out a beam of strong heat.'

Many field-guns, the report said, had been hidden around the country near Horsell Common, and especially between the Woking district and London. Five of the machines had been seen moving towards the Thames and one, by a lucky chance, had been destroyed. In other cases the shells had missed, and the guns had at once been destroyed by the Heat-Rays. Heavy losses of soldiers were mentioned, but in general the report was optimistic.

The Martians had been defeated, my brother read. They had gone back to their cylinders again, in the circle around Woking. Guns, including some very large ones, were moving in quickly. One hundred and sixteen were now in position, mainly covering London. There had never been such a large or fast movement of war equipment in England before.

No doubt, said the report, the situation was strange and serious, but the public was asked to avoid and discourage panic. No doubt the Martians were very frightening, but there could not be more than twenty of them against our millions.

All down Wellington Street people could be seen reading the paper. Men came running from buses to get copies. Certainly people were excited by the news, whatever they had felt before. A map shop in the Strand opened specially, and a man in his

Sunday clothes could be seen inside quickly fixing maps of Surrey to the shop window.

Going along the Strand to Trafalgar Square, my brother saw some of the refugees from West Surrey. There was a man with his wife and two boys and some pieces of furniture in a cart, and close behind him came another one with five or six well-dressed people and some boxes and cases. The faces of the people showed that they were very tired. Some distance behind them was a man on an old-fashioned bicycle. He was dirty and white-faced.

My brother turned towards Victoria station, and met a number of people like these. He had an idea that he might see me. He noticed an unusual number of police controlling the traffic. Some of the refugees were exchanging news with the people on the buses. Most were excited by their strange experience. My brother spoke to several of the refugees but none could give him any news of Woking, except one man who said that it had been totally destroyed the previous night.

At that time there was a strong feeling on the streets that the government should be blamed because they had not destroyed the Martians already.

At about eight o'clock the sound of firing could be heard clearly all over the south of London. My brother walked from Westminster to his room near Regent's Park. He was now very worried about me.

There were one or two carts with refugees going along Oxford Street, but the news was spreading so slowly that Regent Street and Portland Place were full of people taking their usual Sunday night walk. Along the edge of Regent's Park there were as many romantic couples as there had ever been. The night was warm and still. The sound of guns continued from time to time and after midnight there seemed to be lightning in the south.

My brother read and reread the paper, thinking that the worst had happened to me. He was restless, and after supper went out again. He returned and tried to concentrate on his examination notes, but without success. He went to bed a little after midnight and was woken in the early hours of Monday morning by the sound of knocking on doors, feet running in the street, distant drumming and the ringing of bells. For a moment he lay in surprise. Then he jumped out of bed and ran to the window.

Up and down the street other windows were opening and people were shouting questions. 'They are coming!' a policeman shouted back, banging on the door. 'The Martians are coming!' Then he hurried to the next door.

The sound of drums came from the army base in Albany Street and bells were ringing in every church. There was a noise of doors opening, and the lights went on in window after window in the houses across the street.

A closed carriage came up the street, quickly followed by a number of other fast-moving vehicles. Most of them were going to Chalk Farm station, where special trains were being loaded.

For a long time my brother stared out of the window in total surprise, watching the policeman banging at door after door. Then he crossed the room and began to dress, running with each piece of clothing to the window in order to miss nothing of the growing excitement. And then men selling unusually early newspapers came shouting into the street:

'London in danger! Kingston and Richmond defences broken! Terrible killing in the Thames Valley!'

All around him – in the rooms below, in the houses on each side and across the road, and all across London – people were rubbing their eyes and opening windows to stare out and ask questions, and getting dressed quickly as the first breath of the coming storm of fear blew through the streets. It was the beginning of the great panic. London, which had gone to bed on Sunday night not knowing much and caring even less, was woken in the early hours of Monday morning to a real sense of danger.

Unable to learn what was happening from his window, my brother went down and out into the street, just as the sky turned pink with the dawn. Every moment brought more and more fast-moving people in vehicles.

'Black Smoke!' he heard people shouting. 'Black Smoke!'

As he stood at the door, not knowing what to do, he saw another newspaper-seller approaching him. The man was running away with the others and selling his papers for many times their normal price as he ran – a strange mixture of profit and panic.

And from this paper my brother read that terrible report from the commander of the army:

> The Martians are able to send out enormous clouds of black smoke. They have poisoned our gunners, destroyed Richmond, Kingston and Wimbledon, and are moving slowly towards London, destroying everything on the way. It is impossible to stop them. There is no safety from the Black Smoke except by running away.

That was all, but it was enough. All of the six million people who lived in the great city were beginning to move. Soon everybody would be trying to escape to the north.

'Black Smoke!' the voices shouted. 'Fire!'

The bells of the local church rang loudly, a carelessly-driven cart smashed, and people screamed and swore. Yellow lights moved around in the houses. And in the sky above them, the dawn was growing brighter – clear and calm.

He heard people running in the rooms, and up and down the stairs behind him. His neighbour came to the door. She was not properly dressed and her husband followed her, shouting.

As my brother began to realize how serious the situation was, he returned quickly to his room, put all the money he had – about ten pounds – into his pockets and went out again into the streets.

Chapter 8   The Black Smoke

While the curate had sat and talked so wildly to me in the flat fields near Walton, and while my brother was watching the refugees pour across Westminster Bridge, the Martians had started to attack again. As it was reported later, most of them remained busy with preparations in the pit on Horsell Common until nine that night, doing something that produced a great amount of Black Smoke.

But three certainly came out at about eight o'clock. They moved forwards slowly and carefully towards Ripley and Weybridge, and so came in sight of the waiting guns. These Martians moved in a line, perhaps two kilometres apart. They communicated with each other by loud howls.

It was this howling and the firing of the guns at Ripley and Weybridge that we heard at Walton. The Ripley gunners had never been in action before. The guns fired one ineffective shell each, then the soldiers ran away. The Martian, without using his Heat-Ray, walked calmly over their guns.

The Weybridge men, however, were better led or were more experienced. Hidden by a wood, it seems they were not noticed by the Martian nearest to them. They aimed their guns well and fired at a distance of about one kilometre.

The shells exploded all round it, and it was seen to move forwards a few steps, and go down. The guns were reloaded quickly. The fallen Martian used its voice, and immediately a second one answered it, appearing over the trees to the south. It seemed that one of its three legs had been broken. All of the second shells missed the Martian on the ground and, immediately, the other Martians used their Heat-Rays on the guns. The shells blew up, the trees all around the guns caught fire and only one or two of the men escaped.

After this it seemed that the three Martians spoke together, and those who were watching them report that they stayed absolutely quiet for the next half-hour. The fallen Martian crawled slowly out of its machine and began to repair its leg. By about nine it had finished, and the machine was seen to move again.

A few minutes later these three were joined by four other Martians, each carrying a thick black tube. A similar tube was given to each of the three, and the seven spread out at equal distances along a curved line between Weybridge and Ripley.

A dozen signal lights went on as soon as they began to move, warning the waiting guns around Esher. At the same time four of the fighting-machines, also carrying tubes, crossed the river, and two of them, black against the western sky, came into sight of myself and the curate as we hurried along the road to the north.

When he saw them, the curate made a frightened noise and began running, but I knew it was no good running from a Martian and I crawled into some bushes by the side of the road. He looked back and turned to join me.

We heard the distant sound of a gun, then another nearer, and then another. And then the Martian closest to us raised his tube and fired it towards the guns, with a loud bang that made the ground shake. The other one did the same. There was no flash, no smoke, simply a loud noise.

I was so excited by all this that I completely forgot about my personal safety and raised my head out of the bushes. As I did, I heard another bang and something flew fast over my head. I expected at least to see smoke or fire, but there was only the deep-blue sky above and one single star. There had been no explosion, no answer from the guns. Silence returned, and three minutes passed.

'What's happened?' said the curate, standing up.

'I've no idea,' I answered.

I looked again at the Martian, and saw that it was now moving east along the river bank. Every moment I expected a hidden gun to fire at it, but the evening calm was unbroken. The figure of the Martian grew smaller as it moved away, and soon it was hidden by the mist and the coming night. The curate and I climbed higher up the hill and looked around. Towards Sunbury there was something dark, like a hill, hiding our view of the country further away. Then, far across the river, we saw another, similar hill. These hills grew lower and broader as we stared.

I had a sudden thought and looked to the north, and there I saw a third of these cloudy black hills.

Everything had become very still. Far away to the north-east we heard the Martians calling to each other, but our guns were silent.

At the time we could not understand these things, but later I learnt the meaning of these frightening black hills. Each of the Martians, standing in the great curve I have described, had used the tube he carried to fire a large cylinder over whatever hill, wood or other possible hiding-place for guns might be in front of him. Some fired only one of these, some two or more. These broke when they hit the ground – they did not explode – and let out an enormous amount of thick Black Smoke. This rose up in a cloud shaped like a hill, then sank and spread itself slowly over the surrounding country. And it was death to breathe that smoke.

It was heavy, this smoke, so when it began to sink down it behaved like a liquid, running down hills and into the valleys. And where it met with water, or even mist or wet grass, a chemical action took place and it turned into a powder that sank slowly and made room for more.

When the smoke had begun to settle, it stayed quite close to the ground so that even fifteen metres up in the air, on the roofs and upper floors of houses and in high trees, there was a chance of escaping its poison. A man later told me that he had watched from a church roof as the smoke filled his village. For a day and a half he stayed up there, tired, hungry and burnt by the sun before it was safe to come down. But that was in a village where the Black Smoke was allowed to remain until it sank into the ground. Usually, when it had done its work, the Martian cleared the air by blowing steam at it.

They did this to the black clouds near us, as we saw in the starlight from the upper window of an empty house. From there we could see the searchlights on Richmond Hill and Kingston Hill moving in the sky, and at about eleven the windows shook, and we heard the sound of the large guns that had been put in position there. These continued for a quarter of an hour, firing blindly at Martians too far away to be seen. Then the fourth cylinder fell — a bright green star to the north-east.

So, doing it methodically, as a man might kill insects, the Martians spread this strange killing smoke over the country towards London. The ends of the curve slowly moved apart, until at last they formed a line about twelve kilometres long.

All through the night their tubes moved forwards. They never gave the guns any chance against them. Wherever there was a possibility of guns being hidden, they fired a cylinder of Black Smoke at them, and where the guns could be seen they used the Heat-Ray.

By midnight the burning trees along the slopes of Richmond Hill lit up clouds of Black Smoke which covered the whole valley of the Thames, and went as far as the eye could see.

They only used the Heat-Ray from time to time that night, either because they had a limited supply of material for its production or because they did not want to destroy the country, but only to defeat its people. They certainly succeeded. Sunday night was the end of organized opposition to their movement.

After that no group of men would stand against them, because this would mean almost certain death.

You have to imagine what happened to the gunners towards Esher, waiting so tensely in the evening light, because none of them lived to tell the story. You can see the quiet expectation, the officers watching, the gunners waiting with their horses, the groups of local people standing as near as they were allowed, the ambulances and hospital tents with the burnt and wounded from Weybridge. Then came the dull noise of the shots that the Martians fired, and the cylinder flying over the trees and houses and breaking in the neighbouring fields.

You can imagine, too, how they watched as the blackness rose into the sky. The men and horses near it were seen running, screaming, falling down. There were shouts of fear, the guns suddenly left behind, men on the ground struggling to breathe, and the fast spreading of the dark smoke – a silent black cloud hiding its dead.

Before dawn the Black Smoke was pouring through the streets of Richmond. The government, already falling apart, made one last effort. It told the people of London that they had to run away.

Chapter 9   Escape

You can understand the wave of fear that swept through the greatest city in the world at dawn on Monday morning. People ran to the railway stations, to the boats on the Thames, and hurried by every street that went north or east. By ten o'clock the police were finding it hard to keep control.

All the railway lines north of the Thames had been warned by midnight on Sunday, and trains were being filled. Passengers were fighting for standing room in the carriages even at two o'clock in the morning. By three the crowds were so large around the stations that people were being pushed over and walked on. Guns were fired and knives were used. The police who had been sent to direct the traffic, exhausted and angry, were fighting with the people they had been called out to protect.

And as time passed and the engine drivers and firemen refused to return to London, the people turned in growing crowds away from the stations and onto the roads running north. By midday a cloud of slowly sinking Black Smoke had moved along the Thames, cutting off all escape across the bridges. Another cloud came over Ealing, and surrounded a little island of people on Castle Hill, alive but unable to escape.

After trying unsuccessfully to get onto a train at Chalk Farm my brother came out into the road, pushed through the hurrying lines of vehicles, and had the luck to be at the front of a crowd which was taking bicycles from a shop. He got his hands on one. He put a hole in its front tyre while he was pulling it through the broken window, and cut his wrist, but he managed to get away on it. The foot of Haverstock Hill was blocked by fallen horses, but my brother got onto the Belsize Road.

So he escaped from the worst of the panic in London and reached Edgware at about seven. A kilometre before the village the front wheel of the bicycle broke. He left it at the roadside and walked on. People there were standing on the pavement, looking in surprise at the growing crowds of refugees. He succeeded in getting some food at a pub.

My brother had some friends in Chelmsford, and this perhaps made him take the road that ran to the east. He saw few other refugees until he met the two ladies who later travelled with him. He arrived just in time to save them.

He heard their screams and, hurrying round the corner, saw a couple of men trying to pull them out of the little cart which they had been driving, while a third held onto the frightened horse's head. One of the ladies, a short woman dressed in white, was screaming. The other, younger one was hitting the man who held her arm with a whip.

My brother shouted and ran towards them. One of the men turned towards him. Realizing from his face that a fight was unavoidable, and being a good boxer, my brother hit him hard and knocked him back onto the wheel of the cart.

It was no time for fair fighting, and my brother quietened him with a kick, then took hold of the collar of the man who held the younger lady's arm. He heard the horse move forwards and then the third man hit him between the eyes. The man he held pulled himself free and ran off down the road in the direction from which he had come.

Still recovering, my brother found himself facing the man who had held the horse's head, and realized that the cart was moving away along the road. The man, who looked very well built, tried to move in closer, but my brother hit him in the face. Then, realizing that he was alone, he ran along the road after the cart, with the big man behind him. The man who had run away had now stopped and turned and was following my brother at a greater distance.

Suddenly, my brother fell. The big man tripped over him, and when my brother got to his feet he found himself facing both of them. He would have had very little chance if the younger lady had not very bravely stopped the cart and returned to help him. It seemed that she had had a gun all the time, but it had been under her seat when they were attacked. She fired from six metres away, narrowly missing my brother. The less brave of the two attackers ran away, and the other one followed cursing him. They both stopped further down the road, where the third man lay unconscious.

'Take this!' the younger lady said, and she gave my brother the gun.

'Let's go back to the cart,' said my brother, wiping the blood from his lip.

They walked to where the lady in white was struggling to hold the frightened horse. My brother looked back along the road. The robbers had had enough and were moving away.

'I'll sit here,' he said, 'if I may,' and he got up on the front seat. The younger lady sat beside him and made the horse move.

My brother learned that the two women were the wife and younger sister of a doctor living in Stanmore. The doctor had heard about the Martians at the railway station, on his way home from seeing a patient, and had sent them off, promising to follow after telling the neighbours. He said he would catch up with them by about half-past four in the morning, but it was now nearly nine and there was no sign of him.

They stopped and waited for a few hours, but the doctor did not appear. The younger woman suggested that they should move on and catch a train at St Albans. My brother, who had seen the situation at the stations in London, thought that was hopeless. He suggested that they should drive across Essex to the sea at Harwich, and from there get right out of the country.

Mrs Elphinstone – that was the name of the woman in white – refused to listen to his argument, and kept calling for 'George', but her sister-in-law was very quiet and sensible and agreed to my brother's suggestion. So, intending to cross the Great North Road, they went on towards Barnet. As they got closer they saw more and more people, all tired and dirty. They also noticed a long line of dust rising among the houses in front of them. There was a sharp bend in the road, less than fifty metres from the crossroads. When they came out of it Mrs Elphinstone said, 'Good heavens! What is this you are driving us into?'

My brother stopped the horse.

The main road was a boiling stream of people, a river of human beings rushing to the north. A great cloud of dust, white under the strong sun, made everything within five metres of the ground grey and unclear. More dust was raised all the time by the thick crowd of men and women, horses and vehicles.

'Go on! Go on!' the voices said. 'They're coming.'

It seemed that the whole population of London was moving north. There were people of every class and profession, but they were all dusty; their skins were dry, their lips black and cracked, and all of them looked very afraid.

My brother saw Miss Elphinstone covering her eyes.

'Let's go back!' he shouted. 'We cannot cross this.'

They went back a hundred metres in the direction they had come. As they passed the bend in the road, my brother saw a man lying not far away. His face was white and shining. It was clear that he was near death. The two women sat in silence.

Beyond the bend my brother changed his mind. He turned to Miss Elphinstone. 'We must go that way,' he said, and turned the horse round again.

For the second time that day the girl showed her courage. My brother went into the crowd and stopped a horse pulling a cart, while she drove in front of it. In another moment they were caught and swept forwards with the stream of vehicles. My brother, with red whip-marks on his face and hands from the cart's driver, got up into the driving seat.

'Point the gun at the man behind,' he said, giving it to her, 'if he pushes us too hard. No – point it at his horse.'

Then they began to look for a chance of getting to the right side of the road. But as soon as they were in the stream of vehicles, there was little they could do. They were taken through Barnet and were more than a kilometre beyond the centre of the town before they could fight their way across to the other side of the road.

They turned to the east and climbed a hill. There they stopped for the rest of the afternoon, because they were all exhausted.

They were beginning to feel very hungry and the night was cold. In the evening many people came hurrying along the road near their stopping-place, escaping from unknown dangers and going in the direction from which my brother had come.

Chapter 10   The *Thunder Child*

If the Martians had only wanted destruction, they could have killed the whole population of London on Monday, as it moved out slowly through the neighbouring countryside. If one had flown over London that morning, every road to the north or east would have seemed black with moving refugees, every one a frightened and exhausted human being.

None of the wars of history had such an effect – six million people, moving without weapons or food or any real sense of direction. It was the start of the death of the human race.

And over the blue hills to the south of the river, the Martians moved backwards and forwards, calmly spreading their poison clouds over one piece of country and then over another. They destroyed any weapons they found and wrecked the railways here and there. They seemed in no hurry, and did not go beyond the central part of London all that day. It is possible that many people stayed in their houses through Monday morning. It is certain that many died at home, killed by the Black Smoke.

Until about midday there were still many ships on the Thames, attracted by the enormous sums of money offered by refugees. It is said that many who swam out to these ships were pushed away and drowned. At about one o'clock in the afternoon, the thin remains of a cloud of Black Smoke was seen coming through London's Blackfriars Bridge. This caused a terrible panic and all the ships and boats tried to leave at the same time. Many became stuck together under Tower Bridge, and the sailors had to fight against people who tried to get on from the riverside. People were actually climbing down onto the boats from the bridge above.

When, an hour later, a Martian walked down the river, there was nothing but broken pieces of boats in the water.

I will tell you later about the falling of the fifth cylinder. The sixth one fell in Wimbledon. My brother, watching beside the women in the cart in the field, saw the green flash of it far beyond the hills. On Tuesday the three of them, still intending to get out to sea, drove through the busy country towards Colchester.

That day the refugees began to realize how much they needed food. As they grew hungry, they began to steal. Farmers defended their animals and crops with guns in their hands. A number of people now, like my brother, were moving to the east, and some were even so desperate that they turned back towards London to get food. These were mainly people from the northern suburbs who had only heard of, but not seen, the Black Smoke.

My brother heard that about half the members of the government had met in Birmingham, in central England, and that enormous amounts of explosive were being prepared to be used in the Midlands. He was told that the Midland Railway Company had started running trains again, and was taking people north from St Albans. There was also a notice which said that within twenty-four hours bread would be given to the hungry people. But this did not change their plans, and they continued travelling east. They heard no more about the bread than this notice, and nobody else did either.

That night the seventh cylinder fell in London, on Primrose Hill.

On Wednesday my brother and the two women reached Chelmsford, and there a number of people, calling themselves the Council of Public Safety, took their horse for food. Although the three of them were hungry themselves, they decided to walk on.

After several more hours on the road, they suddenly saw the sea, and the most amazing crowd of ships of all types that it is possible to imagine.

After the sailors could no longer come up the Thames, they went to the towns on the Essex coast to take people onto their ships. Close to the shore was a large number of fishing-boats from various countries, and steamboats from the Thames. Beyond these were the larger ships – a great number of coal ships, ships carrying goods, and neat white and grey passenger ships from Southampton and Hamburg.

About three kilometres out there was a warship. This was the *Thunder Child*, the only one in sight, but far away to the right a column of smoke marked the position of other warships. These waited in a long line, ready for action, right across the mouth of the Thames, watching the Martian attack but powerless to prevent it.

At the sight of the sea Mrs Elphinstone panicked. She had never been out of England before; she would rather die than be friendless in a foreign country. She had been growing increasingly upset and depressed during the two days' journey. Her great idea was to return to Stanmore. Things had always been safe in Stanmore. They would find George in Stanmore.

It was very difficult to get her down to the beach, where after some time my brother caught the attention of some men from a steamboat. They sent a small boat and agreed on a price of thirty-six pounds for the three passengers. The steamboat was going, these men said, to the Belgian port of Ostend.

It was about two o'clock when my brother got onto it with the two women. There was food available, although the prices were very high, and the three of them had a meal.

There were already around forty passengers on the boat, some of whom had spent their last money getting a ticket, but the captain stayed until five in the afternoon, picking up passengers until the boat was dangerously crowded. He would probably have stayed longer if the sound of guns had not begun at about that time in the south. The *Thunder Child*, too, fired a small gun and sent up a string of flags. Some smoke rose as its engines started. At the same time, far away in the south-east, the shapes of three warships appeared, beneath clouds of smoke.

The little steamboat was already moving out to sea, when a Martian appeared, small and far away, moving along the muddy coast from the south. The captain swore at the top of his voice at his own delay, and the ship increased speed.

It was the first Martian that my brother had seen, and he stood, more amazed than frightened, as it moved steadily towards the ships, walking further and further into the water. Then, far away, another appeared, stepping over some small trees, and then another could be seen even further away, crossing the flat mud that lay between the sea and the sky.

Looking to the north-east, my brother saw the long line of ships already moving away from the approaching terror. One ship was passing behind another; many were turning. Steamships whistled and sent up clouds of steam, sails were let out and small boats rushed here and there. He was so interested in this that he did not look out to sea. And then a quick movement of the steamboat (which had turned to avoid being hit) threw him off the seat on which he had been standing. There was shouting all around him, a movement of feet and a cheer that seemed to be answered.

He got to his feet and saw to the right, less than a hundred metres away, the warship cutting through the water at full speed, throwing enormous waves out on either side.

Some water came over the side of the steamboat and blinded my brother for a moment. When his eyes were clear again, the warship had passed and was rushing towards the land. He looked past it at the Martians again and saw the three of them now close

47

together, and standing so far out to sea that their legs were almost completely under water.

It seemed to him that they were surprised by this new enemy. To their minds, perhaps, no other machine could be as large as themselves. The *Thunder Child* fired no gun, but simply sailed at full speed towards them. Probably because it did not fire, it managed to get quite close. They did not know what it was. If the ship had fired one shell, they would have sent it straight to the bottom with the Heat-Ray.

Suddenly, the nearest Martian lowered his tube and fired a cylinder at the *Thunder Child*. This hit its left side and sent up a black cloud that the ship moved away from. To the watchers on the steamboat, low in the water and with the sun in their eyes, it seemed that the warship was already among the Martians.

They saw the three thin figures separating and rising out of the water as they moved back towards the shore, and one of them raised the box that fired his Heat-Ray. He held it pointing down, and a cloud of steam came up from the water as it hit the ship.

A flame rose up through the steam and then the Martian began to fall over. In another moment it had hit the sea, and a great amount of water and steam flew high in the air. The guns of the *Thunder Child* were heard going off one after another, and one shot hit the water close by the steamboat.

No one worried about that very much. As the Martian fell, the captain shouted and all the crowded passengers at the back of the steamer joined in. And then he shouted again. Because, rushing out beyond the smoke and steam came something long and black with flames coming from it.

The warship could still turn and its engines worked. It went straight towards a second Martian, and was within a hundred metres of it when the Heat-Ray hit it. There was a violent bang, a blinding flash and the warship blew up. The Martian was thrown back by the violence of the explosion, and in another moment the burning wreckage, still moving forwards, had broken the Martian like something made of wood. My brother shouted. A boiling cloud of steam hid everything again.

'Two!' shouted the captain.

Everyone was shouting and they could hear shouts and cheers from the other ships and the boats. The steam stayed in the air for many minutes, hiding the third Martian and the coast. All this time the steamboat was moving steadily out to sea and away from the fight, and when at last the steam cleared, the black cloud got in the way and they could see nothing of either the *Thunder Child* or the third Martian. But the other warships were now quite close and moving in towards the shore.

The little ship my brother was on continued to move out to sea, and the warships became smaller in the distance.

Then suddenly, out of the golden sunset, came the sound of guns and the sight of black shadows moving. Everyone moved to the side of the steamboat and looked to the west, but smoke rose and blocked the sun. Nothing could be seen clearly. The ship travelled on while the passengers wondered.

The sun sank into grey clouds, the sky darkened and an evening star came into sight. Then the captain cried out and pointed. Something rushed up into the sky, something flat and broad and very large, and flew in a great curve. It grew smaller, sank slowly and disappeared again into the night. And as it flew, it rained down darkness on the land.

Chapter 11   Earth Under the Martians

In the last two chapters I have moved away from my own adventures to tell of the experiences of my brother. All through this time I and the curate had been hiding in the empty house where we went to escape the Black Smoke. We stayed there all Sunday night and all the next day – the day of the panic – in a little island of daylight, cut off by the Black Smoke from the rest of the world. We could only wait and be bored during those two days.

I was very worried about my wife. I thought of her in Leatherhead, frightened, in danger, thinking of me already as a dead man. I knew my cousin was brave enough for any emergency, but he was not the sort of man to understand danger quickly and do something about it. These worries stayed on my mind and I grew very tired of the curate's constant talking. After trying and failing to keep him quiet, I kept away from him in other rooms in the house.

We were surrounded by the Black Smoke all that day and the following morning. There were signs of people in the next house on Sunday evening – a face at a window and moving lights, and later the closing of a door. But I do not know who these people were or what happened to them. We saw nothing of them the next day. The Black Smoke moved slowly towards the river all through Monday morning, slowly getting nearer and nearer to us, coming at last along the road outside the house that hid us.

A Martian walked across the fields at about midday, killing the stuff with steam. When we looked out I saw the country covered with black dust, but we were no longer trapped. As soon as I saw that escape was possible, my dream of action returned. But the curate did not want to leave.

'We are safe here – safe here,' he repeated.

I decided to leave him. The soldier had taught me well and I looked for food and drink and a spare shirt to take with me. When it was clear to the curate that I intended to go alone, he suddenly decided to come. Everything was quiet through the afternoon and we started at about five o'clock along the blackened road to Sunbury.

Here and there along the road, and in Sunbury itself, were dead bodies of horses as well as men, turned-over carts and luggage, all covered thickly with black dust. As we passed other small towns, we found them unaffected by either Heat-Ray or Black Smoke, and there were some people alive, although none could give us news. Here too, there were signs of quick departure. I remember a pile of three broken bicycles, flattened by the wheels of passing carts. We crossed Richmond Bridge at about half-past eight. Once again, on the Surrey side, there was black dust that had once been smoke, and some dead bodies – a number of them near the approach to the station.

Then suddenly, as we walked north, we saw some people running. The top of a Martian fighting-machine came into sight over the house tops, less than a hundred metres away from us. We stood shocked by our danger, and if the Martian had been looking down we would have died immediately. We were too frightened to go on and hid in a hut in a garden. There the curate lay down, crying silently and refusing to move again.

But my fixed idea of reaching Leatherhead would not let me rest, and in the evening I went out again. I left the curate in the hut, but he came hurrying after me.

That second start was the most foolish thing I ever did. It was obvious that the Martians were all around us. As soon as the curate caught up with me, we saw either the fighting-machine we had seen before or another one, far away across the fields. Four or five little black figures hurried in front of it, and in a moment it became obvious that this Martian was hunting them. In three steps it was among them, and they ran away in all directions. It did not use its Heat-Ray, but picked them up one by one and threw them into a large metal box which stuck out behind it.

For the first time, I realized that perhaps the Martians had another purpose, apart from destroying human beings. We stood for a moment in terror, then ran through a gate behind us into a garden and hid in a corner until the stars were out.

It was nearly eleven o'clock before we felt brave enough to go out again. We kept away from the road, moving through gardens and some areas full of trees. When we got to Sheen, the curate said that he felt unwell and we decided to try one of the houses.

The one we chose was in a walled garden, and in the kitchen we found some food. There were two loaves of bread, a raw steak and some cooked meat. Under a shelf we found some bottled beer, and there were two bags of green beans and some lettuce. In a cupboard there was some tinned soup and fish and two tins of cake. I am listing these exactly because we lived on this food for the next fortnight.

We sat in the kitchen in the dark and had a meal of cold food, and just before midnight there was a blinding flash of green light followed by the loudest bang I have ever heard. There was a crash of glass, the sound of falling walls, and then the ceiling fell down in pieces on our heads. I was knocked across the floor and my head hit the oven. I lay there unconscious for a long time, the curate told me, and when I woke up he was wiping my face with a wet handkerchief.

For some time I could not remember what had happened.

'Are you better?' he asked.

At last I answered him. I sat up.

'Don't move,' he said. 'The floor is covered with broken plates. You can't possibly move without making a noise, and I think *they* are outside.'

We both sat in complete silence, so we could hardly hear each other breathing. Outside and very near was the noise from a machine, which started and stopped.

'What is it?' I asked.

'A Martian!' said the curate.

Our situation was so strange and unbelievable that for three or four hours, until the dawn came, we hardly moved. And then the light came, not through the window, which was filled with earth from the garden, but through a small hole that had been knocked in the wall. Through this we saw the body of a Martian, watching a cylinder which was still red with heat. When we saw that, we moved as slowly as possible out of the grey light of the kitchen and into the darkness of the hall.

Suddenly, the truth came to me.

'The fifth cylinder!' I whispered. 'It's hit this house and buried us under the ruins!'

For a time the curate was silent, then he said, 'God help us!'

For hours we lay there in the darkness, while from outside came the sounds of hammering and then, after some time, a sound like an engine. Towards the end of the day I found that I was very hungry. I told the curate that I was going to look for food, and moved back into the kitchen again. He did not answer, but as soon as I began eating I heard him crawling towards me.

After eating we went back to the hall, and I fell asleep. When I woke up and looked around I was alone. I crawled back into the kitchen and saw him lying down and looking out of the hole at the Martians.

The noises still continued. Through the hole I could see the top of a tree, turned to gold by the evening sun. I stepped carefully through the broken plates that covered the floor.

I touched the curate's leg, and he moved so suddenly that some bricks slid down outside with a loud crash. I took hold of his arm, afraid that he might cry out, and for a long time we remained still. Then I raised my head cautiously to see what had happened. The falling bricks had left another hole in the wall of the building. Through this I was able to see into what had been, only the previous night, a quiet road. Things had changed greatly.

The fifth cylinder had not fallen on our house, but on top of the house next door. The building had completely disappeared. The cylinder had gone right through it and made a large hole in the ground, much larger than the pit I had looked into in Woking. The earth all around had been thrown up over the neighbouring houses. Our house had fallen backwards. The front part of it had been destroyed completely. By chance the kitchen had escaped and now stood buried under earth and bricks, covered on every side except towards the cylinder. We now lay on the very edge of the enormous round pit that the Martians were making.

The cylinder was already open in the centre of the pit, and on the furthest side one of the great fighting-machines, empty now, stood tall and unmoving against the evening sky. However, at first I hardly noticed the pit and the cylinder, because of the strange shining machine that I saw working there, and the odd creatures that were crawling slowly and painfully across the earth near it.

This machine was shaped like a spider with five legs and a great number of tentacles. With these it was taking pieces of metal out of the cylinder and laying them on the earth behind it. It was doing this so quickly and perfectly that I did not see it as a machine at first. The fighting-machines were extraordinary, but could not compare to this building-machine. People who have never seen these things can hardly understand how alive they looked.

I had seen the Martians themselves once before, but only for a short time, and then the sight had almost made me sick. Now I was more used to them, and was in a good position with a lot of time to study them properly. They were the strangest creatures it is possible to imagine. They had large, round bodies – or perhaps heads – about a metre and a half across. Each body had a face in front of it. This face had no nose – I do not think they had any sense of smell – but it had a pair of very large, dark eyes, and just beneath these a kind of v-shaped mouth. In the back of the head, or body – I do not really know what to call it – there was a flat surface like the skin of a drum, which we now know worked as an ear. Around the mouth were sixteen thin, whip-like tentacles, arranged in two groups of eight. These worked like hands.

As I watched the Martians, they seemed to be trying to raise themselves on the hands, but with their increased weight on Earth this was impossible. It may be that on Mars they moved around on them quite easily.

Most of the space inside their bodies was taken by the brain. Besides this they had a heart, but they had no stomach because they did not eat. Instead, they took fresh blood from living creatures and used a tube to put it straight into their own bodies. This idea seems horrible to us, but at the same time I think we should remember how disgusting our meat-eating habits would seem to an intelligent rabbit.

In three other ways their bodies were different from ours. They did not sleep, and because they had very simple bodies they never seemed to get tired. On Earth they could not move without effort, but even at the end of their time here they remained active. In twenty-four hours they did twenty-four hours of work.

Also, strange as it may seem, the Martians were absolutely without sex. A young Martian, we now know, was born on Earth during the war, and it was found growing out of the body of its parent, just like some young plants.

A final difference seems very unimportant. Germs, which cause so much disease and pain on Earth, have either never appeared on Mars or they got rid of them a long time ago.

It is generally supposed that the Martians communicated by sounds and by moving their arms. But no human being saw as much of them as I did and lived to tell the story, and I can say that I have seen four, five or six of them slowly performing the most difficult work without sound or any other signal. I know a little of psychology and I am absolutely certain that they exchanged thoughts.

While I was still watching their slow movements in the sunlight, the curate pulled violently at my arm. I turned and saw an unhappy face and silent, moving lips. He wanted to see what was happening. The hole was only big enough for one of us to look through, so I had to stop watching them for a time while he had his chance.

When I looked again, the busy building-machine had already put together several of the pieces of metal from inside the cylinder into a shape that was very like its own. Down on the left a busy little digging-machine could be seen, sending out small clouds of green smoke and working its way round the pit, making it bigger and piling the earth up over the top. This was what had caused the regular beating noise. It whistled as it worked, and no Martian seemed to be controlling it.

Chapter 12   In the Ruined House

The arrival of a second fighting-machine made us move back out of the kitchen into the hall, because we were afraid that from that height the Martian might see us through the hole. At a later date we began to feel less in danger of being seen because the sunlight outside was very bright, but at first anything approaching the house drove us back into the hall in fear. However, despite the danger, we could not prevent ourselves from going back to look again and again. In our desire to watch, we even fought each other within a few centimetres of being seen.

We were very different people with different habits of thought and action, and those differences increased because we were living together in this dangerous place. The curate talked endlessly, and this prevented me from forming a plan of action.

He had no self-control at all and sometimes cried for hours at a time. He ate more than I did, and did not seem to understand that we had to stay in the house until the Martians had finished their work if we wanted to stay alive. I tried threatening him, and in the end I hit him. That worked for some time.

The curate was watching through the hole when the first men were brought there. I was sitting near him, listening hard. He made a sudden movement backwards and for a moment I shared his panic. Then curiosity gave me courage and I got up, stepped across him and went to the hole.

At first I could see no reason for his behaviour. The night was coming but the Martians had lights on their machines. The whole scene was one of moving lights and shadows, difficult for the eyes. The Martians at the bottom of the pit could no longer be seen, because the earth around it was now so high. A fighting-machine stood in the corner of the pit. Then, through the noise of the machinery, came the faint sound of human voices.

I watched the fighting-machine closely, sure for the first time that it did actually contain a Martian. I could see the oily shine of its skin and the brightness of its eyes. And suddenly I heard a shout and saw a long tentacle reaching over the shoulder of the machine to the little cage on its back. Then something – something struggling violently – was lifted high against the sky and brought down again. I saw that it was a man. He was fat, red-faced, middle-aged, well-dressed; perhaps earlier he had been important. He disappeared behind the pile of earth and for a moment there was silence. Then we heard him scream and the sound of long and cheerful calling from the Martians.

I moved away from the hole, put my hands over my ears and ran into the hall. The curate, who had been lying silently with his arms over his head, looked up as I passed, cried out quite loudly and came running after me.

That night, as we hid in the hall, I felt a great need to do something but could think of no plan of escape. But afterwards, during the second day, I was able to consider our position clearly. The curate, I found, was quite unable to discuss anything. The death of the man outside had taken away all his powers of thought. He had almost sunk to the level of an animal. I began to think that, although our position was terrible, there was no reason yet to give up hope. The Martians might only stay in this pit for a short time, then move on. Or if they stayed permanently, they might not think it necessary to watch it all the time.

On the third day, if I remember correctly, I saw a boy killed. It was the only occasion on which I actually saw the Martians feed. After that I avoided the hole in the wall for most of a day.

The Martians had made such an impression on me that at first I did not think I could escape. I did not think that they could be defeated by human beings. But on the fourth or fifth night I heard a sound like heavy guns.

It was very late and the moon was shining brightly. The Martians had taken away the digging-machine and apart from the fighting-machine on the far side of the pit and a building-machine that was busy out of my sight, the pit was empty. I heard a dog, and that familiar sound made me listen. Then I heard a noise exactly like the sound of big guns. I heard six bangs and then six more. And that was all.

On the sixth day of our imprisonment I looked out for the last time, and I soon found myself alone. Instead of staying close and trying to move me away from the pit, the curate had gone back into the hall. I followed him quickly and quietly and in the darkness I heard him drinking. I put my hand out and my fingers closed around a bottle of wine.

For a few minutes we fought together. The bottle hit the floor and broke, and I stopped fighting and got up. We stood breathing heavily, staring at each other. In the end I moved between him and the food and told him that I was going to take control.

58

I divided the food in the cupboard into separate amounts to last us ten days. I would not let him eat any more that day. In the afternoon he tried to get some food. I had been asleep but in a moment I was awake. All day and all night we sat face to face. I was tired but would not give up, and he cried and complained about his immediate hunger. The rest of the time he just talked to himself, and I began to realize that he had gone completely mad.

Through the eighth and ninth days his voice grew louder. He threatened me, begged me, and this was mixed with a great deal of talk about his service to God. Then he slept for some time and began again with even more strength, so loudly that I had to try to stop him.

'Be still!' I demanded.

He rose to his knees. 'I have been still too long,' he said, loud enough for the Martians to hear, 'and now I must tell the world. This place will be destroyed because of the bad things we have done!'

'Shut up!' I said, getting to my feet. 'Please —'

'No!' he shouted, at the top of his voice. 'Speak! The word of God is with me!'

In three steps he was at the door leading to the kitchen.

I went after him, picking up the coal-hammer as I entered the room. Before he was half-way across the floor, I was right behind him. I swung the hammer and hit him on the back of the head. He fell forwards and lay flat on the floor. I stepped over him and stood there breathing hard. He did not move.

Suddenly, I heard a noise outside and the hole in the wall became dark. I looked up and saw the lower part of a building-machine coming slowly across it. Then, through a sort of glass plate, I saw the large, dark eyes of a Martian, and one of its tentacles appeared, moving in through the hole.

I turned, tripped over the curate and stopped at the hall door. The tentacle was now two metres or more into the room, moving backwards and forwards with strange, sudden movements. I forced myself back into the hall. I shook violently and could hardly stand straight. Had the Martian seen me? What was it doing now?

Then I heard the sound of a heavy body – I knew whose it was – being dragged across the floor of the kitchen towards the opening. I could not stop myself – I moved to the door and looked back into the kitchen. In the light from outside, I saw the Martian studying the curate's head. I thought at once that it would know that I was there from the mark of the hammer.

I shut the door and moved back into the hall and tried to hide myself in the corner. Then I heard a faint metallic sound as the tentacle moved back across the kitchen floor. I thought that it might not be long enough to reach me. I prayed. Then I heard it touching the handle. It had found the door. The Martians understood doors!

It moved the handle up and down for a moment, and then the door opened.

In the darkness I could just see the thing moving towards me and examining the wall and the floor. It was like a black snake moving its head from side to side.

Once, even, it touched my boot. I almost screamed, but I bit my hand. For a time it did not move, then it moved back through the door.

I heard it go into the food cupboard. It moved the tins and a bottle broke. Then there was silence.

Had it gone?

At last I decided that it had.

The tentacle did not come into the hall again, but I lay all the tenth day in the darkness, too frightened even to move for a drink. I did not enter the kitchen again for two days. When at last I did, I found that the food cupboard was now empty. The Martians had taken everything. On that day and the next I had no food and nothing to drink.

On the twelfth day my thirst was so bad that I went into the kitchen and used the noisy rainwater pump that stood by the sink. I managed to get a couple of glasses of dirty water. This made me feel a lot better, and the noise of the pump did not bring a tentacle in through the opening.

On the thirteenth day I drank some more water, and thought of impossible plans of escape. Whenever I slept, I dreamed either of the death of the curate or of wonderful dinners.

Then, early on the fifteenth day, I heard the sound of a dog outside. This greatly surprised me. I went into the kitchen and saw its head looking in through the hole.

I thought that if I could attract it in quietly, I would be able, perhaps, to kill and eat it. It would be a good idea to kill it anyway, in case its actions attracted the attention of the Martians.

I moved forwards, saying, 'Good dog!' very softly, but it suddenly pulled his head back and disappeared.

I listened. I heard the sound of some birds but that was all.

For a long time I lay close to the opening until, encouraged by the silence, I looked out.

Except in the corner, where a number of birds fought over some dead bodies, there was not a living thing in the pit.

I stared around, hardly believing my eyes. All the machinery had gone. Slowly I made the opening larger and pushed myself through it. I could see in every direction except behind me and there were no Martians in sight.

I hesitated, then with a rush of desperate courage, and with my heart beating violently, I climbed to the top of the pile of earth in which I had been buried.

When I had last seen this part of Sheen, it had been a street of comfortable white and red houses. Now the neighbouring ones had all been destroyed. Far away I saw a thin cat walking along a wall, but there was no sign of people.

After my time in the darkness, the day seemed very bright, the sky a shining blue. A gentle wind moved the flowers. And oh! the sweetness of the air.

For some time I stood there, not worrying about my safety. At that moment, I felt the beginning of something that soon grew quite clear in my mind, that worried me for many days. I was not the master now, but an animal among the animals, under the power of the Martians. The rule of man had ended.

But as soon as this feeling came, it left me, and my main problem became hunger. I climbed a wall and fell into a neighbouring garden. Here I found some young vegetables, which I took. Then I started walking towards the river. There were two ideas in my mind – to get more food and to move, as quickly as possible, away from the pit.

When I reached the Thames, I drank as much water as I could. I then walked up a hill to Putney Common.

Here I moved through areas which had been totally destroyed and others which were totally undamaged; houses with their curtains and their doors closed. I went into a couple of the houses, looking for food, but all of it had already been taken. I lay for the rest of the day in a garden, too exhausted to go on.

All this time I saw no human beings and no signs of the Martians. I saw a couple of hungry-looking dogs, but they hurried away from me. I also saw some human bones, with all the flesh eaten off. After sunset I struggled on along the road towards Putney, and in a garden I found some potatoes, enough to stop my hunger. From there I looked down on Putney and the river.

The view of blackened trees and empty ruined buildings made me very unhappy. And over all – silence. It filled me with terror to think how quickly that great change had come. Near the top of Putney Hill I came across more human bones, eaten clean and left lying around. The Martians, it seemed, had killed and eaten everyone around there, except for a few lucky ones like myself. They were now looking for food somewhere else. Perhaps even now they were destroying Berlin or Paris, or maybe they were moving north.

Chapter 13   The Man on Putney Hill

I spent that night in the pub that stands on the top of Putney Hill, sleeping in a made bed for the first time since I had run away to Leatherhead. I broke into the house – and afterwards found that the front door was unlocked. I searched every room for food until, when I was ready to give up, I found some bread and two tins of fruit in one of the bedrooms. The place had already been searched and emptied. Later, in the bar, I found some sandwiches that no one had noticed. I ate some of these and put the rest in my pockets.

I lit no lamps, afraid that a Martian might come through that part of London looking for food in the night. Before I went to bed I was very restless and went from window to window, looking out for some sign of them. I slept little. As I lay in bed, I found myself thinking of the killing of the curate.

I had no regrets about this, but in the stillness of the night, with a sense that God was near, I thought again of every part of our conversation from the time we had first met. We had been unable to co-operate. If I had known, I would have left him at Walton, but I had not been able to see ahead. Nobody saw me kill him, but I have described it here and the reader can make a judgement.

The morning was bright and fine and there were little golden clouds in the eastern sky. In the road that runs from the top of Putney Hill to Wimbledon many things had been left behind by the crowds that ran towards London on the Sunday night after the fighting began. There was a little two-wheeled cart with a broken wheel. It had the name of a shop written on it. There was a hat lying in the mud, and a lot of broken glass with blood on it.

I moved slowly because I was very tired and my plans were uncertain. I had an idea of going to Leatherhead, although I knew there was little chance of finding my wife there. Certainly, unless they had been killed, she and my cousins would have run away.

I came to the edge of Wimbledon Common and stood there, under cover of some trees and bushes. It stretched far and wide and I hesitated on the edge of that large open space. Soon I had an odd feeling of being watched and, turning suddenly, I saw something hiding in some of the bushes. I took a step towards it, and it rose up and became a man armed with a sword. I approached him slowly. He stood silently, watching me but not moving.

As I came nearer, I saw that he was dressed in clothes as dusty and dirty as my own. His black hair fell over his eyes, and his face was dark and dirty and thin, so at first I did not recognize him.

'Stop!' he cried, when I was within ten metres of him, and I stopped. 'Where have you come from?' he said.

I thought, watching him.

'I have come from Sheen,' I said. 'I was buried near the pit the Martians made around their cylinder. I have escaped.'

'There is no food around here,' he said. 'This is my country: all this hill down to the river and up to the edge of the common. There is only food for one. Which way are you going?'

'I don't know,' I said.

He looked at me uncertainly, then his expression suddenly changed. He pointed at me.

'It's you,' he said, '– the man from Woking. And you weren't killed at Weybridge?'

I recognized him at the same moment.

'You're the soldier who came into my garden.'

'What luck!' he said. 'We are lucky ones!' He put out a hand and I took it. 'I hid,' he said. 'But they didn't kill everyone. And after they went away, I went towards Walton across the fields. But – it's only been sixteen days and your hair is grey.' He looked over his shoulder suddenly. 'Only a bird,' he said. 'This *is* a bit open. Let's crawl under those bushes and talk.'

'Have you seen any Martians?' I asked. 'Since I got out –'

'They've gone away across London,' he said. 'I guess they've got a bigger camp there. The night before last I saw some lights up in the air. I believe they've built a flying-machine and are learning to fly.'

I stopped, on hands and knees, because we had come to the bushes.

'Fly!'

'Yes,' he said, 'fly!'

I crawled into an open space in the bushes and sat down.

'If they manage to do that, we haven't got a chance,' I said. 'They will simply go round the world.'

'They will. But it will make things easier around here. And besides . . .' he looked at me. 'Don't you believe that we're beaten? I do.'

I stared. Strange as it may seem, I had not thought of things this way, although it was perfectly obvious. I had still held onto some hope.

'It's finished,' he said. 'They've lost *one* – just *one*. And they've taken over the capital of the most powerful country in the world. The death of that one at Weybridge was an accident. And these are only the first ones. They keep coming. These green stars – I've seen none for five or six days, but I've no doubt they're falling somewhere every night. There's nothing we can do. We're beaten!'

I did not answer. I sat staring in front of me, trying without success to find a way of arguing against him. Suddenly, I remembered the night I had watched through the telescope.

'After the tenth shot they fired no more – at least until the first cylinder came.'

'How do you know?' said the soldier. I explained. 'Something wrong with the gun?' he said. 'But even if there is, they'll get it right again.'

We sat looking at each other.

'And what will they do with us?' I said.

'That's what I've been thinking.' he said. 'It seems to me that at the moment they catch us when they want food. But they won't keep doing that. As soon as they've destroyed all our guns and ships and railways, they'll begin to catch us one by one, picking the best and keeping us in cages and things. They haven't begun on us yet. Don't you see that?'

'Not begun!' I cried.

'Not begun. And instead of rushing around blindly, we've got to change to suit the new situation. That's how I see it.'

'But if that's true,' I said, 'what is there to live for?'

'There won't be anything important for a million years or more – no music, no art and no nice little visits to restaurants. No entertainment. But men like me are going to go on living – so human beings can continue. And if I'm not mistaken, you'll show how strong you are too. We aren't going to be killed. And I don't intend to be caught, either, and caged and fattened. Ugh!'

'You don't mean –'

'I do. I'm going on. Under their feet. I've thought about it. We've got to learn while we've got a chance. And we've got to live and stay independent while we learn. That's what has to be done.'

I stared, surprised and greatly affected by the man's courage.

'Good God!' I said. 'You are a brave man.' And suddenly I held his hand. 'Go on,' I said.

'Well, people who intend to escape them must get ready. I'm getting ready. But not all of us can live like animals, and that's how we'll have to live. That's why I watched you. I had my doubts. You're thinner. I didn't know that it was you, you see. All these – the sort of people that lived in these houses, all those little office workers that used to live down that way – they'd be no good. They haven't any spirit in them – no proud dreams and no great ideas. They just used to rush off to work – I've seen hundreds of them, with a bit of breakfast in their hand, running to catch their train, frightened they'd be sacked if they didn't. Well, the Martians will be a good thing for them. Nice big cages, fattening food, no worry. After a week or two running around the fields on empty stomachs they'll come and be caught quite happily.' He paused. 'The Martians will probably make pets of some of them; train them to do tricks – who knows? And some, maybe, they will train to hunt us.'

'No,' I cried, 'that's impossible! No human being –'

'What's the good of going on with such lies?' said the soldier. 'There are men who would do it cheerfully. What nonsense to pretend there aren't!'

And I realized that I agreed with him.

I sat and thought about these things. It was interesting that he, an ordinary soldier, seemed to have a much better understanding of the situation than I, a professional writer.

'What plans do you have?' I said.

He hesitated.

'Well, we have to invent a life where people can live and have children, and be safe enough to bring the children up. Yes – wait a bit, and I'll make it clearer what I think ought to be done. The ones the Martians capture will be like farm animals; in a few years they'll be big, beautiful, stupid – rubbish. But we who stay free risk turning into wild animals.

'You see, I intend to live underground. I've been thinking about the drains. Under London there are hundreds of kilometres of them. And we can dig passages between the drains and buildings. And then there are the railways, where they go underground. You begin to see? And we'll get some people together – strong, clean-minded men. We're not going to accept any rubbish that comes in. Weak ones go out again.'

'As you intended me to go?'

'Well – I discussed it, didn't I?

'We won't argue about that. Go on.'

'The people who stay will obey orders. We want strong, good women too – mothers and teachers. No lazy ones with rolling eyes. We can't have any weak or silly ones. Life is real again, and the useless and bad ones have to die. They ought to die. They ought to be willing to die. It would be wrong of them to live and weaken the others.

'But it's no good just staying alive. That's just living like rats. We have to save our knowledge, and add to it. That's why men like you are needed. We must make great safe places deep underground, and get all the books we can; not novels and poetry, but ideas, science books. We must go to the British Museum and choose the best books in it. Especially, we must keep our science – learn more.'

The soldier paused and laid a brown hand on my arm.

'In fact, it may not be so difficult to learn how their fighting-machines work. Think of four or five of them with men inside, firing Heat-Rays back at the Martians!'

For some time the imagination of the soldier, and the confidence and courage he showed, persuaded me completely. I believed in his idea of the future and in the possibility of his plans. We talked like this through the early morning, and later came out of the bushes. After checking the sky for Martians, we hurried quickly to the house on Putney Hill where he had his hiding-place.

There I saw the work he had spent a week on. It was a passage about ten metres long, designed to reach the main drain on Putney Hill. For the first time I began to think that there was some distance between his dreams and his powers, because I could dig a hole like this in a day. But I believed in him enough to work with him all that morning at his digging.

As we worked I thought about the job, and soon some doubts began to come into my mind. I thought about the distance to the drain and the chances of missing it completely. I also felt that it would be easier to get into the drain and dig back towards the house. And just as I was beginning to face these things, the soldier stopped digging and looked at me.

'We're working well,' he said. 'Let's stop. I think it's time we looked around from the top of the house.'

I wanted to continue, but a thought came to me.

'Why were you walking around on the common,' I asked, 'instead of being here?'

'Taking the air,' he said. 'It's safer by night.'

'But the work?'

'Oh, one can't always work,' he said, and in a flash I understood the man clearly.

We went together to the roof and stood on a ladder, looking out of the roof door. No Martians could be seen. We went back down into the house. Neither of us wanted to start digging again, and when he suggested a meal I was quite happy to agree.

Afterwards we drank wine and played cards. He won most of the games, and when we did not want to play any more I went back up on the roof.

I stayed there for a long time, looking north over the city. I began to feel that I had failed my wife, and decided to leave this dreamer of great things and to go on into London. There, it seemed to me, I had the best chance of learning what the Martians and human beings were doing.

Chapter 14   Dead London

After I had said goodbye to the soldier, I went down the hill, along the High Street and across the bridge to Fulham. There was black dust on the road after the bridge, and it grew thicker in Fulham. The streets were horribly quiet. I found some old bread in a baker's shop there. After that, the streets became clear of powder and I passed some white houses which were on fire. The noise of burning was actually better than silence.

Beyond Fulham the streets were quiet again. Here I found more black powder and some dead bodies. I saw about ten along Fulham Road. They had been dead for many days, so I hurried quickly past them. The black powder covered them and softened their shapes. One or two had been partly eaten by dogs.

Where there was no black powder, it was curiously like Sunday in the financial area of London, with the closed shops, the houses locked up and the curtains closed. In some places thieves had been at work, but usually only at the food and wine shops. A jeweller's window had been broken open in one place, but the thief had clearly been chased away, because a number of gold chains and a watch were lying on the pavement. I did not take the trouble to touch them. Further down the road, a woman in torn clothes was sitting on a doorstep. The hand that hung over her knee was cut, and blood had fallen onto her dirty brown dress. A broken bottle of wine had formed a pool on the pavement. She seemed asleep, but she was dead.

The silence grew greater. But it was not the stillness of death – it was the stillness of expectation. At any time the destruction that had already happened to the north-western borders of the city, that had destroyed Ealing, might strike among these houses and leave them smoking ruins. It was an empty city waiting for death . . .

In South Kensington the streets were clear of dead people and of black powder, and near there I first heard the howling. It started very quietly. It was a sad movement between two notes, 'Ulla, ulla, ulla, ulla,' continuing without stopping. When I passed streets that ran to the north it grew louder, and then houses and buildings seemed to cut it off again. It came most loudly down Exhibition Road. I stopped, staring towards Kensington Gardens.

It seemed that all the empty houses had found a voice for their fear and loneliness.

'*Ulla, ulla, ulla*,' cried that inhuman note – great waves of sound sweeping down the broad, sunlit road, between the tall buildings on each side. I turned to the north, towards the iron gates of Hyde Park. The voice grew stronger and stronger, although I could see nothing above the roof-tops on the north side of the park except some smoke to the north-west.

'*Ulla, ulla, ulla*,' cried the voice, coming, it seemed to me, from the district around Regent's Park. The howl affected my mind, and my mood changed. I also found that I was very tired, and hungry and thirsty again.

It was already past midday. Why was I walking alone in this city of the dead? I thought of old friends that I had forgotten for years. I thought of the poisons in the chemists' shops, the bottles in the wine shops . . .

I came into Oxford Street by Marble Arch, and here again were black powder and several bodies. After a lot of trouble, I managed to break into a pub and find some food and drink. I was tired after eating and went into the room behind the bar and slept on a black leather sofa that I found there.

I awoke to find that sad howling still in my ears: '*Ulla, ulla, ulla, ulla, ulla.*' It was now getting dark, and after I had found some bread and cheese in the bar I walked on through the silent squares to Baker Street and so came at last to Regent's Park. And as I came out of the top of Baker Street, I saw far away over the trees, in the clearness of the sunset, the top of the Martian fighting-machine from which this howling came. I was not frightened. I watched it for some time, but it did not move. It appeared to be standing and calling, for no reason that I could discover.

I tried to work out a plan of action. That non-stop sound of '*Ulla, ulla, ulla, ulla*' confused my mind. Perhaps I was too tired to be very afraid. Certainly I was more curious to know the reason for this howling. I turned and went into Park Road, intending to go round the edge of the park, with houses between us to keep me safe, and get a view of this unmoving, howling Martian from the direction of St John's Wood.

I came to a destroyed building-machine halfway to St John's Wood station. At first I thought a house had fallen across the road, but when I climbed up on the ruins I saw, with a shock, this great machine lying, with its tentacles bent and twisted, among the ruins that it had made. The front part of it was pushed in. It seemed that it had been driven blindly straight at the house, and had been turned over when the house fell on it.

Wondering about all that I had seen, I moved on towards Primrose Hill. Far away, through a space in the trees, I saw a second Martian fighting-machine, as unmoving as the first, standing in the park near the Zoo. Then the sound of '*Ulla, ulla, ulla, ulla*' stopped. The silence came suddenly. And now night, the mother of fear and mystery, was coming.

London around me looked like a city of ghosts. My imagination heard a thousand noiseless enemies moving. Terror came to me. In front of me the road became black and I saw the twisted shape of a body lying across the pavement. I could not go on. I turned down St John's Wood Road and ran away from this terrible stillness.

I hid from the night and the silence until long after midnight, in a garden hut in Harrow Road. But before dawn my courage returned, and while the stars were still in the sky I turned again towards Regent's Park. I lost my way among the streets, and soon saw down a long road, in the half-light of the early dawn, the curve of Primrose Hill. There, on the top, high against the early morning stars, was a third Martian, standing still like the others.

A mad idea came to me. I would die and end it. And I would save myself even the trouble of killing myself. I marched on without fear towards this great machine, and then, as I came nearer and the light grew, I saw that a number of black birds were circling and gathering around the top of it. I began to feel very happy and I started running along the road.

I got onto the grass before the sun rose. Great piles of earth had formed around a pit at the top of the hill – the final and largest one the Martians had made – and from behind these piles thin smoke rose against the sky. Against the sky-line an eager dog ran and disappeared. The thought that had flashed into my mind grew real, and believable. I felt no fear, only a wild, shaking excitement, as I ran up the hill towards the unmoving Martian. Out of the top of it hung long, brown pieces of flesh, which the birds were tearing away.

In another moment I had climbed a pile of earth and stood on its top, and the pit was below me. It was a large space, with enormous machines here and there within it, great piles of material and strange buildings. And all around it, some in their overturned war-machines and some in building-machines, and ten of them lying in a row, were the Martians – *dead!* They had been killed by germs against which their systems could not fight; killed, after all man's machines had failed, by the smallest things that God has put on this Earth.

It had happened in this way, and I and many others did not see that it would happen because terror and disaster had blinded our minds. These germs of disease have killed people and animals since the beginning of time, but over these many years we have developed the ability to fight against them. But there are no germs on Mars, and as soon as the Martians arrived, as soon as they drank and fed, our tiny friends began to destroy them. By paying with a million lives, human beings have bought their right to live on Earth. It is our home and would be ours even if the Martians were ten times as strong as they are.

I stood staring into the pit, and my heart grew wonderfully happy as the rising sun lit up the world around me. The pit was still in darkness. Only the tops of the great engines, so unearthly in their shape, could be seen in the morning light. I heard a large number of dogs fighting over the bodies that lay in the darkness at the bottom of the pit.

Across the pit, on its further edge, lay the great flying-machine which they had been testing in our heavier atmosphere when disease and death stopped them. Death had not come a day too soon. At the sound of birds overhead I looked up at the enormous fighting-machine that would never fight again, at the pieces of red flesh that dropped down onto the overturned seats on the top of Primrose Hill.

I turned and looked down the slope of the hill at those two other Martians that I had seen the previous night. They were surrounded by birds now. One of them had died as it had been crying to its friends. Perhaps it was the last to die, and its voice had gone on and on until its machinery stopped. They stood now, harmless tripods of shining metal, against the brightness of the rising sun.

All around the pit, and saved from everlasting destruction, lay the great city. And as I looked at it, and realized that the shadows had been rolled back, and that people might still live in its streets, and that this dear city of mine might be once more alive and powerful again, I felt such emotion that I was very close to tears.

The trouble had ended. That same day the healing would begin. People who were still alive would start to return, and life would come back to the empty streets. The sound of tools would soon be heard in all the burnt and broken houses. At the thought, I lifted my hands towards the sky and began thanking God. In a year, I thought, we would rebuild all that had been destroyed.

Then came the thought of myself, of my wife, and the old life of hope and tender helpfulness that had ended forever.

Chapter 15   Wreckage

And now comes the strangest thing in my story. But perhaps it is not totally strange. I remember, clearly and in great detail, all that I did that day until the time when I stood crying on the top of Primrose Hill. And then I forget.

I know nothing of the next three days. I have learned since then that I was not the first discoverer of the Martian defeat – several wanderers like me had already known about it on the previous night. One man – the first – had even managed to send a telegram to Paris. From there the happy news had flashed all over the world; a thousand cities, living in great fear, suddenly turned on all their lights.

They knew of it in Dublin, Edinburgh, Manchester and Birmingham at the time when I stood on the edge of the pit. Already men, crying with joy, as I have heard, were getting onto trains to go to London. Men on bicycles rode through the countryside shouting the news to all.

And the food! Across the Channel, across the Irish Sea, across the Atlantic, corn, bread and meat were coming to us. All the ships in the world seemed to be coming to London in those days. But I have no memory of all of this. For three days I walked aimlessly, a madman. Then I found myself in a house of kind people, who had found me. They have told me since that I was singing a crazy song about 'The Last Man Left Alive! The Last Man Left Alive!' Although they were troubled with their own affairs, these people were very helpful to me. They gave me a place to stay and protected me from myself.

Very gently, when my mind was working again, they told me all they knew about what had happened in Leatherhead. Two days after I was imprisoned it had been destroyed, with every person in it, by a Martian. He had swept it all away for no reason at all, it seemed.

I was a lonely man, and they were very kind to me. I was a sad one too, and they were patient with me. I stayed with them for four days after my recovery. All that time I felt a growing need to look again at whatever remained of the little life that had seemed so happy and bright in my past. My hosts tried to change my mind but at last, promising faithfully to return to them, I went out again into the streets that had lately been so dark and strange and empty.

Already they were busy with returning people; in places there were even shops open. I remember how bright that day seemed as I went sadly back to the little house in Woking – how busy the streets were, and how full of life. But then I noticed how ill the people looked and how many of them still wore old and dirty clothes. The churches were giving out bread sent to us by the French government, and tired-looking policemen stood at the corners of every street.

At the end of Waterloo Bridge I bought a copy of the first newspaper to reappear. I learned nothing new except that already in one week the examination of the Martians' machines had produced amazing results. Among other things, the newspaper said that the 'Secret of Flying' had been discovered. I did not believe this at the time.

At Waterloo I found that free trains were taking people to their homes. The first rush had already ended and there were few people on the train. The city we went through was dirty with the powder of the Black Smoke, despite two days of thunderstorms and rain.

All down the line from there, the country looked empty and unfamiliar. Wimbledon particularly had suffered, and beyond there I saw piles of earth around the sixth cylinder. A number of people were standing by it, and some soldiers were busy in the middle. Over it was a British flag, flying cheerfully in the wind.

The line on the London side of Woking station was still being repaired, so I got off the train at Byfleet and took the road to Maybury, past the place where I had seen the Martian fighting-machine in the thunderstorm. I was curious and I stopped to find the twisted and broken dog-cart with the whitened bones of the horse. For a time I stood and looked at the remains . . .

Then I returned through the wood towards my home. A man standing at the open door of a house greeted me by name as I passed. I looked at my own house with a quick flash of hope that died immediately. The door had been broken, and it was opening slowly as I approached.

It blew shut again. The curtains of my study blew out of the open window from which I and the soldier had watched the dawn. No one had closed it since then. I went into the hall, and the house felt empty. The stair carpet was discoloured where I had sat, wet to the skin from the thunderstorm on that first terrible night. Our muddy footsteps still went up the stairs.

I followed them to my study and found, lying on my writing-table, the page of work I had left on the afternoon of the opening of the cylinder. For some time I stood reading it. I remembered how I could not concentrate that morning, hardly a month before, and how I had stopped work to get my newspaper from the newsboy. I remembered how I went to the garden gate as he came past, and how I had listened to his odd story of 'Men from Mars'.

I came down and went into the dining-room. There were the remains of the meat and the bread, now gone bad, where the soldier and I had left them. My home was a lonely place. I realized the stupidity of the small hope I had held on to for so long. And then a strange thing happened.

'The house is deserted,' said a voice. 'No one has been here for ten days. Don't stay here and make yourself unhappy. No one escaped except you.'

I was shocked. Had I spoken my thought aloud? I turned, and

the door to the garden was open behind me. I took a step towards it and stood looking out.

And there, amazed and afraid, as I too stood amazed and afraid, were my cousin and my wife – my wife white and tearless. She gave a faint cry.

'I came here,' she said. 'I knew – knew –'

She put her hand to her throat and started to fall. I stepped forwards and caught her in my arms.

♦

I can only regret now, as I finish my story, how little I can help with the many questions which are still unanswered. In one area I shall certainly be criticized. I know very little about medical matters, but it seems to me most likely that the Martians were killed by germs.

Certainly, in all the bodies of the Martians that were examined after the war, no germs were found except ones that came from Earth. Besides this, we still know very little about the Black Smoke, and the way that the Heat-Ray worked remains a puzzle.

A question of more serious interest is the possibility of another attack from the Martians. I do not think that nearly enough attention is being paid to this. Every time the planet Mars comes near to us, I worry that they might try again. We should be prepared. It should be possible to find the position of the gun from which the shots came, to watch this part of the planet carefully and be ready.

In that case, the cylinder could be destroyed before it was cool enough for the Martians to come out, or they could be killed by guns as soon as the door opened. It seems to me that they have lost a great advantage in the failure of their first surprise. Possibly they also believe this.

One astronomer has given excellent reasons for supposing that the Martians have actually landed on Venus. Seven months ago, when these planets were close together, faint, dark marks appeared on photographs which suggested that a cylinder had been fired from one to the other.

However, whether we expect another attack or not, our views of the human future must now be changed by these events. We have learned that we cannot think of this planet as a safe home for humans. We can never know what unseen good or evil might come to us suddenly out of space. Perhaps this attack from Mars will be helpful to us in the end. It has taken away our confidence in the future, which was making us soft; it has given great help to science, and it has made us think of human beings as one family.

Perhaps, across the great distances of space, the Martians have watched what happened to the ones that landed on Earth and learned their lesson – and have found a safer home on the planet Venus. Even if that is true, for many years we will continue to watch Mars carefully, and all falling stars will make us afraid.

The war has broadened people's minds enormously. Before it there was a general belief that there was no life in space apart from on our tiny planet. If the Martians can reach Venus, there is no reason to think that this is impossible for us. So when the slow cooling of the sun means that we cannot continue to live on Earth, it may be that life which began here can reach out and continue there.

But that is a distant dream. We may, on the other hand, still be destroyed by the Martians. The future may belong to them and not to us.

I must admit that the trouble and danger of our time have left a continuing sense of doubt and fear in my mind. I sit in my study writing by lamplight, and suddenly I see the valley below on fire again, and feel that the house around me is empty and lonely. I go out into the Byfleet Road, and vehicles pass me, a boy on a bicycle, children going to school – and suddenly they become strange and unreal, and I hurry on again with the soldier through the hot, dangerous silence. At night I see the black powder darkening the silent streets, and the twisted bodies covered by it. They stand up in front of me, torn and dog-bitten. They talk and grow angry, paler, uglier, and I wake, cold and shaking, in the darkness.

I go to London and see the busy crowds in Fleet Street and the Strand, and it comes to my mind that they are just the ghosts of the past, walking the streets that I have seen silent and empty, spirits in a dead city. And it is strange, too, to stand on Primrose Hill, as I did only a day before writing this last chapter. I saw the houses stretching away and disappearing into the smoke and mist, people walking up and down between the flower-beds, and the sightseers around the Martian machine that still stands there. I heard the noise of playing children and remembered the deep silence of the dawn of that last great day . . .

And it is strangest of all to hold my wife's hand again, and to think that I have thought of her, and that she has thought of me, among the dead.

ACTIVITIES

Chapters 1–3

Before you read

1 Look at the Word List at the back of the book and answer these questions.

    a Are *germs visible* if you look at them through a *telescope*?

    b When there is a sudden *threat* of terrible *destruction*, do people *panic*?

    c Are *astronomers* interested in the laws of *gravity* and in *meteorites*?

2 Writing at the end of the nineteenth century, H. G. Wells had to think of a way for the Martians to travel. Which of these methods do you think he uses to send their spaceship from Mars to Earth?

    a It is fired out of a large gun.

    b It uses a jet engine, which burns gas.

    c It uses the sun's energy.

3 Find London, the grey area, on the map facing page 1.

    a Is Woking south or north of London?

    b Is Barnet south or north of London?

    c Which is closer to London, Richmond or Stanmore?

While you read

4 What information does the writer give us in Chapter 1? Are these sentences true (T) or false (F)?

    a Mars is cooler and darker than Earth. .....

    b Mars is older than Earth. .....

    c Mars is seven times larger than Earth. .....

    d Martians are not as intelligent as people on Earth. .....

    e Mars will soon be too cold for life to continue there. .....

5 Ogilvy, the astronomer, is the first person to see the Martian cylinder. Number these events, 1–6, in the order that they happen in Chapter 2.

    a He realizes that the cylinder is hollow.   .....

    b He runs to Woking.   .....

    c He hears movement.   .....

    d He tries to help the thing in the cylinder.   .....

    e He climbs down into the pit.   .....

    f He meets some local people.   .....

6 Circle the correct words as you read Chapter 3.

    a The Thing from Mars is the shape of a *meteorite / cylinder*.

    b When the lid falls onto the sand, everyone expects to see a *Martian / man*.

    c The big, greyish round creatures have long *heads / tentacles*.

    d A group of men with a white flag approach the pit because they want to *talk to / kill* the creatures.

    e The Martians kill many men with their *ray of light / swords*.

    f The writer says that he runs from the common, crying silently and full of terror of the Martians and the *fires / stillness* around him.

After you read

7 Discuss how the writer's feelings about his own safety change in this part of the book. Why?

8 In Wells's opinion, how do people behave when they are faced with an unknown threat? Do you agree or disagree with him?

9 Work with another student. Have this conversation.

    Student A: You are the writer at the end of Chapter 3. Make a phone call to a newspaper and describe what has happened.

    Student B: You are a reporter at the newspaper. Ask questions to get the full story.

Chapters 4–6

Before you read

10 Which of these sentences describe what will happen next, do you think?

   a As the news of the deaths on the common spreads, people panic and start to run away.

   b The writer has to leave his home because of the Martian threat.

   c The Martians build large fighting-machines and kill more people.

   d The army attacks the Martians and moves them back from London.

   e There are no more arrivals from Mars.

   f The Martians want to speak to people in the government in London.

While you read

11 In which order, 1–8, do these events happen in Chapter 4?

   a A company of soldiers comes through Horsell and spreads out around the common. .....

   b The writer reads inaccurate descriptions in the newspapers about the deaths of Stent, Henderson, Ogilvy and the others. .....

   c The writer meets some engineers under the railway bridge and they ask him questions. .....

   d People in Chertsey fire guns into the wood where the second cylinder has fallen. .....

   e The writer arrives home and tells his shocked wife what he has seen. .....

   f The Martians destroy the Oriental College, so the writer decides to leave the town with his wife and servant. .....

   g A second cylinder falls from the sky. .....

   h People who crawled near the Martians' pit are killed by their invisible light-ray. .....

12 Are these sentences true (T) or false (F)?

    a The writer thinks that London will be safe.   .....

    b The officer believes everything that the soldier and
        the writer tell him.   .....

    c People in Byfleet are packing and getting ready to
        leave town when the writer arrives there.   .....

    d The writer tells others to jump into the river because
        he wants to save them from the terrible Heat-Ray.   .....

    e After the creature's head explodes, it continues
        marching and knocks down a church tower.   .....

After you read

13 Who is speaking, and to whom? What are they talking about?

    a 'It's no kindness to your wife for you to get killed.'

    b 'You are the first people I've seen coming this way this
        morning.'

    c 'I was explaining that these are valuable.'

    d 'You have been asking for water for the last hour.'

    e 'Things have changed! You must stay calm. There is still hope.'

Chapters 7–9

Before you read

14 Discuss these questions.

    a The events in the early part of the story have taken place
        southwest of London. What do you think will happen in Chapter
        7?

    b How will the government react to the Martians, do you think?

    c How will news of their arrival spread?

While you read

15 Circle the correct ending for each sentence.

    a The Martians communicate with each other by
       howling.   a humming.   waving their tentacles.

    b The more experienced fighters are the men from
       Ripley.   Walton.   Weybridge.

    c When the writer and the curate see the fighting machines, the
       writer
       begins running.   crawls into some bushes.   fires a gun.

    d The cylinders inside the Martians' tubes contain
       water.   missiles.   poisonous smoke.

    e The writer and the curate escape to
       an empty house.   a hospital tent.   London.

    f By Sunday night, the people, the organized opposition and the
       government are
       beginning to win the battle.   defeated by the Martians.
       all dead.

16 What happens to the writer's brother? Match the two halves of
these sentences.

    a After he tries unsuccessfully to get on a train at
       Chalk Farm, …   .....

    b After he leaves the bicycle with the broken front
       wheel, …   .....

    c After he tries to rescue two women and has a fight, …   .....

    d After he hears the women's plans to catch a train at
       St Albans, …   .....

    e After he gets the women through Barnet, …   .....

    1) he manages to persuade the younger woman to drive to
       Harwich and leave the country.

    2) he is given a gun by the younger woman.

    3) he manages to take a bicycle from a shop.

    4) he manages to turn to the east and climb a hill.

    5) he manages to get some food at a pub.

After you read

17 Discuss the way the news of the Martians was reported in the newspapers and how the public reacted. How were six million Londoners informed of the attack?

18 How well do you think the British government handled this attack from Mars? Would a modern government be better prepared in a situation of this type?

19 Work with another student. Have this conversation.

Student A: You are the writer's brother. You have reached the hill with the two women and you are exhausted. It is evening and someone who is going in the direction from which you came has stopped. Answer his/her questions from your own experience and from what people are saying.

Student B: You are on your way to Barnet. Ask the writer's brother questions about what he saw there. Try to get as much information from him as you can.

Chapters 10–12

Before you read

20 Chapter 10 begins: *If the Martians had only wanted destruction, they could have killed the whole population of London on Monday.* Why didn't they, do you think?

While you read

21 Answer these questions. Write YES or NO.

a Are people trying to escape London along the Thames?   .....

b Does the writer's brother watch the sixth cylinder fall on Primrose Hill?   .....

c Does the writer's brother give the horse to the Council of Public Safety?   .....

d Is the *Thunder Child* the only warship?   .....

e Does the writer's brother see a Martian as the steamboat moves out to sea?   .....

f Is the *Thunder Child* blown up by the Martians' Heat-Ray?   .....

g Does the Martians' spaceship disappear into the night sky?   .....

22 Complete this description of the Martians with information from Chapter 11.

The Martians have large, ... bodies, about one and a half metres across. They have very large .... and a small mouth, but no .... They have something like an ear – only one – on the .... of their heads. Inside, they have a very large brain and a .... , but there is no .... because they don't eat. Instead, they take in fresh .... from a tube.

There are three other differences between Martians and humans. First, Martians never .... Second, they don't have sex; a new Martian grows from the side of an old one. And third, they communicate by ....

23 In the ruined house, who

    a goes completely mad?   ....

    b hits the curate with a hammer?   ....

    c drags the curate's body across the kitchen floor?   ....

    d opens the kitchen door with the handle?   ....

    e takes all the food from the kitchen?   ....

After you read

24 Answer these questions.

    a How do refugees get onto the ships in the Thames?

    b How do the refugees get food?

    c What does the writer's brother think the Martians feel when they see the *Thunder Child*? Why does he think this?

Chapters 13–15

Before you read

25 Will the writer find his wife and brother, do you think? Will the Martians be defeated in the end? If so, how?

26 The writer meets a soldier with a plan for living under the Martians. Which of these (✓) are part of his plan?

   a live underground   .....

   b eat people who are weak   .....

   c use drains to travel between buildings   .....

   d use underground trains   .....

   e leave weak people to die   .....

   f get a lot of poetry books   .....

   g get a lot of science books   .....

27 What happens to the writer? Put these events in order, 1–8.

   a The writer returns to his home.   .....

   b He finds a lot of dead Martians in a pit.   .....

   c People return to London.   .....

   d He hears odd sounds coming from the Martian machines.   .....

   e His wife and family find him again.   .....

   f The writer goes to central London and finds the streets empty.   .....

   g He realizes that the Martians have been killed by germs.   .....

   h A kind family look after him.   .....

After you read

28 On Wimbledon Common, the soldier describes his ideas for a group of people who will continue to live free of the Martians. He talks about 'strong, clean-minded men and women' who are prepared to obey orders. How do you feel about his ideas for a future society? What rules would you make for a society like this?

29 In *The War of the Worlds*, which was written in 1898, Wells suggests certain weapons that might be used in the future. These include fighting-machines, flying machines, heat-rays and poison gas.

   a How accurate were his ideas about the future of war?

   b Do you think people will continue to invent new ways of killing, or will weapons of war become unnecessary?

Writing

30 The Martians have landed in Woking. Write the newspaper story that appears in a London paper just after they first land. You do not want to frighten the public and you do not know what will happen next.

31 How does Wells persuade his readers that this attack is a 'real' possibility? What advice can you give to new writers of science fiction stories who want to write persuasively? Write a list of suggestions.

32 Write a description of Wells's Martians and their fighting-machines for a magazine about creatures from Mars.

33 Write a comparison of the actions and behaviour of the soldier and the curate. Why do you think Wells created these characters? What was his message?

34 Write a letter from the writer's brother to the writer. Tell him what happened to you and what you saw during that terrible month.

35 The writer says that he has no regrets about the curate's death. Write his letter to the police explaining the situation in the ruined house, the action he took and his reasons for his lack of regret.

36 After the Martians are dead, life begins to return to normal, but it will never be quite the same again. Write an interview between you and the (fictional) writer. How does he think people's ideas about life, Earth and other planets will change after this attack from Mars?

37 There have been many books since this one about wars between different planets. Why do you think Wells's novel is still very popular?

38 Choose one or two characters from the story and write what you would have done differently if you had been them. Explain why.

39 Did you enjoy this novel? Why (not)? Give your opinions.

WORD LIST

astronomer (n) a scientist who studies the stars and planets

carriage (n) a vehicle for people that is pulled by a horse

cart (n) a vehicle for goods that is pulled by a horse

column (n) something with a tall, narrow shape

common (n) a large public area of grass in a village or town

crawl (v) to move on your hands and knees

curate (n) a priest whose job is to help another priest

cylinder (n) a container with round ends and straight sides

destruction (n) the process of destroying something

drain (n) a pipe that carries waste liquids away

edition (n) the first or later printing of a newspaper

germ (n) a very small living thing that can make you ill

gravity (n) the force that makes objects fall to the ground

howl (n) a long, loud crying sound

hum (n) a low, continuous sound

meteorite (n) a small piece of rock moving through space

missile (n) a weapon that can fly over long distances

panic (n/v) a sudden, strong feeling of fear

pit (n) a hole that has been dug in the ground

ray (n) a narrow beam of light or energy

refugee (n) someone who has been forced to leave their country or their home

shell (n) an exploding container that is fired from a gun

slope (n) a piece of ground that is higher at one end

telegram (n) a message sent by an early method, using electricity

telescope (n) an instrument used to see distant objects

tentacle (n) a long arm, like the arms of some sea creatures

threat (n) the possibility that something bad will happen

tripod (n) a piece of equipment with three legs

visible (adj) that can be seen or noticed

whip (n) a long, thin piece of leather with a handle

The Talented Mr Ripley
Patricia Highsmith

Tom Ripley goes to Italy. He needs to find Dickie Greenleaf.
Dickie's father wants him to go back to America. But Tom likes
Italy, and he likes Dickie's money. Tom wants to stay in Italy, and
he will do anything to get what he wants. *The Talented Mr Ripley*
is now an exciting movie with Matt Damon, Gwyneth Paltrow and
Jude Law.

Ripley's Game
Patricia Highsmith

One night, Tom Ripley is insulted by a man at a party. An ordinary
person would just be upset by this, but Tom Ripley is not an
ordinary person. Months later, when a friend asks him for help with
two simple murders, he remembers this night and plans revenge.
He starts a game – a very nasty game, in which he plays with the
life of a sick and innocent man. But how far will he go?

A Time to Kill
John Grisham

Ten-year-old Tonya Hailey is attacked and raped by two local men.
Carl Lee, Tonya's father, shoots them. Now only his lawyer and
friend, Jake Brigance, stands between him and the electric chair. Is
there a legal defense for Carl Lee's actions?

*There are hundreds of Penguin Readers to choose from – world classics,
film adaptations, modern-day crime and adventure, short stories,
biographies, American classics, non-fiction, plays ...*

For a complete list of all Penguin Readers titles, please contact your local
Pearson Longman office or visit our website.

Longman Dictionaries

Express yourself with confidence!

Longman has led the way in ELT dictionaries since 1935. We constantly talk to students and teachers around the world to find out what they need from a learner's dictionary.

Why choose a Longman dictionary?

Easy to understand

Longman invented the Defining Vocabulary – 2000 of the most common words which are used to write the definitions in our dictionaries. So Longman definitions are always clear and easy to understand.

Real, natural English

All Longman dictionaries contain natural examples taken from real-life that help explain the meaning of a word and show you how to use it in context.

Avoid common mistakes

Longman dictionaries are written specially for learners, and we make sure that you get all the help you need to avoid common mistakes. We analyse typical learners' mistakes and include notes on how to avoid them.

Innovative CD-ROMs

Longman are leaders in dictionary CD-ROM innovation. Did you know that a dictionary CD-ROM includes features to help improve your pronunciation, help you practice for exams and improve your writing skills?

For details of all Longman dictionaries, and to choose the one that's right for you, visit our website:

www.longman.com/dictionaries